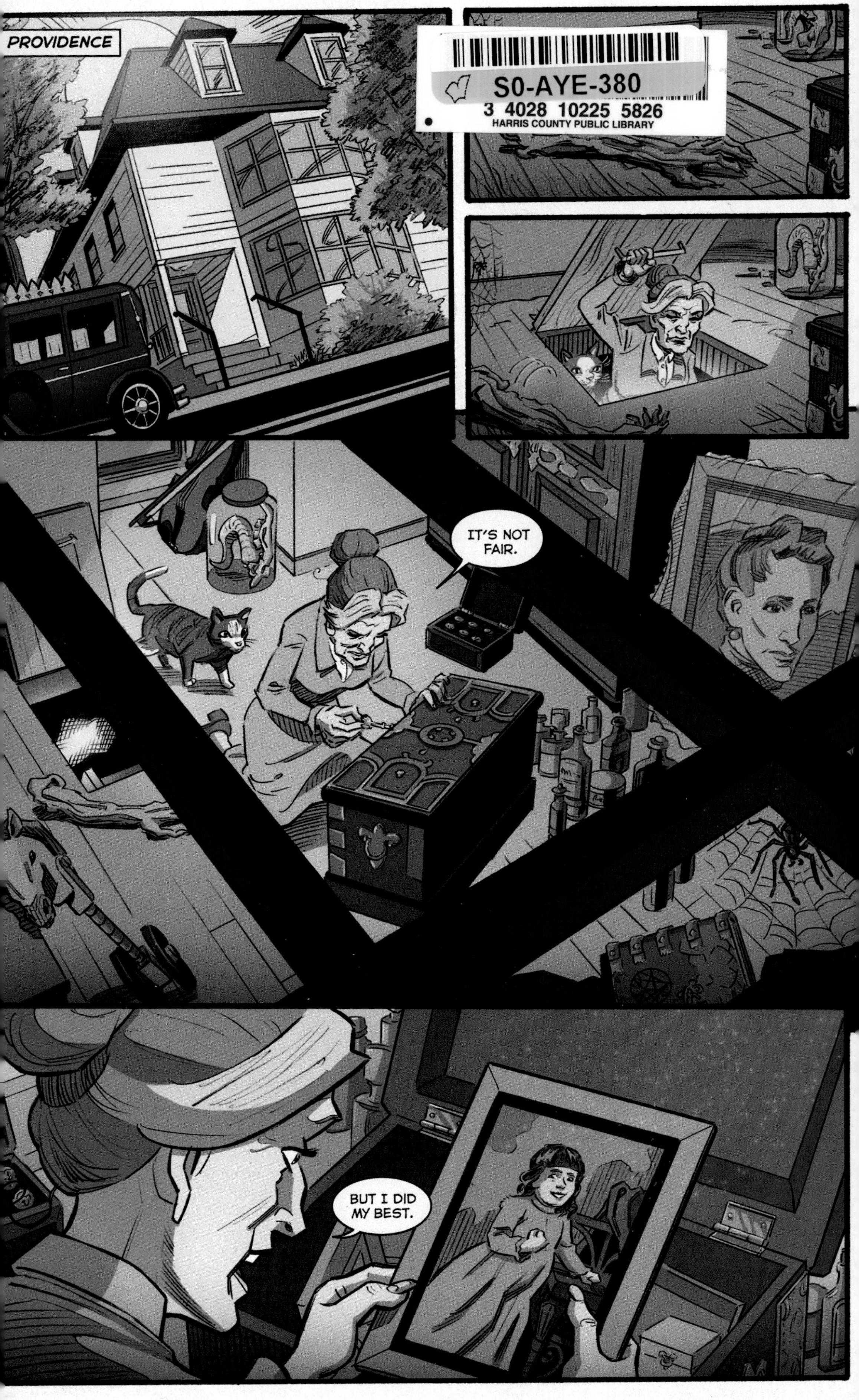
PROVIDENCE
IT'S NOT FAIR.
BUT I DID MY BEST.

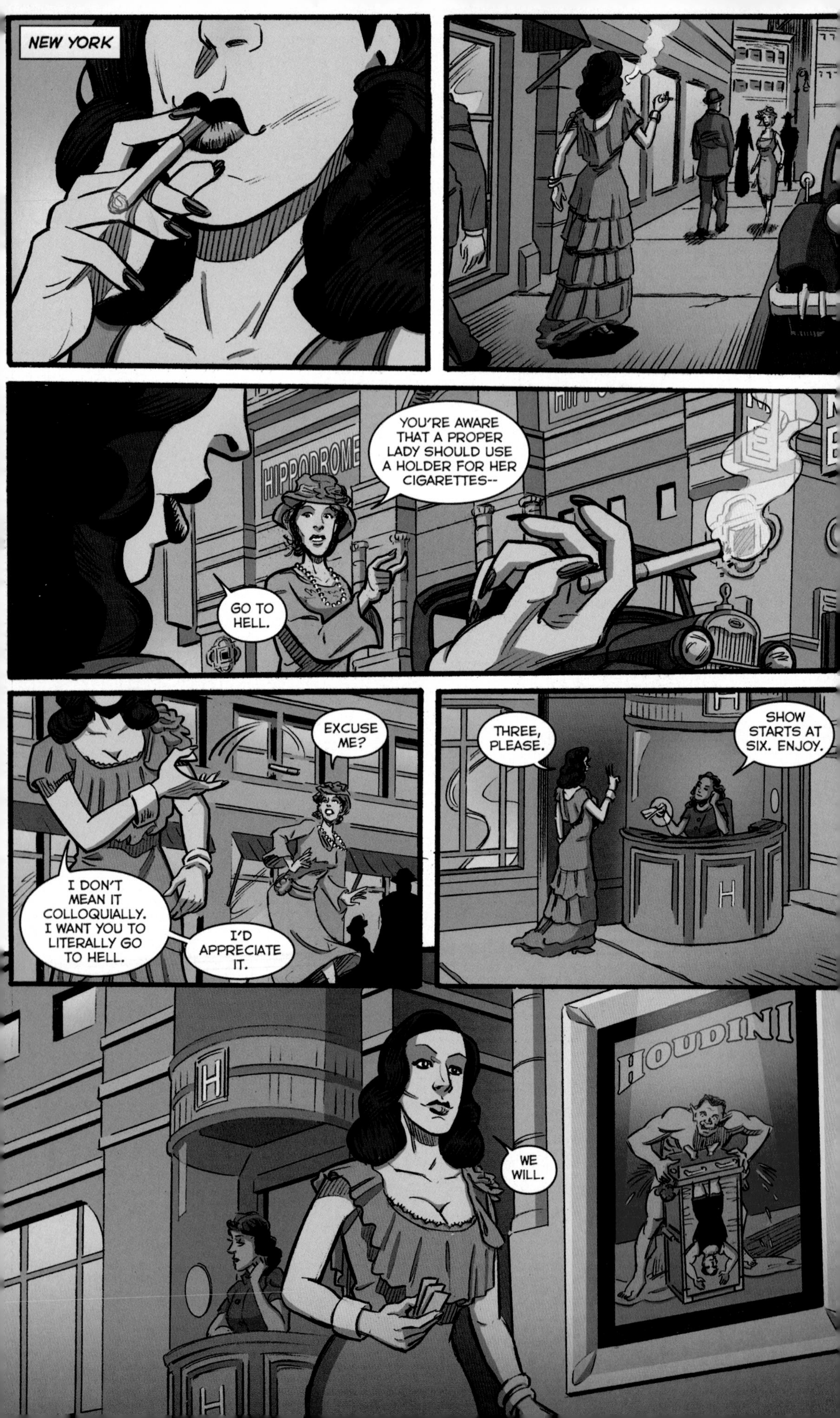
NEW YORK
YOU'RE AWARE THAT A PROPER LADY SHOULD USE A HOLDER FOR HER CIGARETTES--
GO TO HELL.
HIPPODROME
EXCUSE ME?
I DON'T MEAN IT COLLOQUIALLY. I WANT YOU TO LITERALLY GO TO HELL.
I'D APPRECIATE IT.
THREE, PLEASE.
SHOW STARTS AT SIX. ENJOY.
WE WILL.
HOUDINI

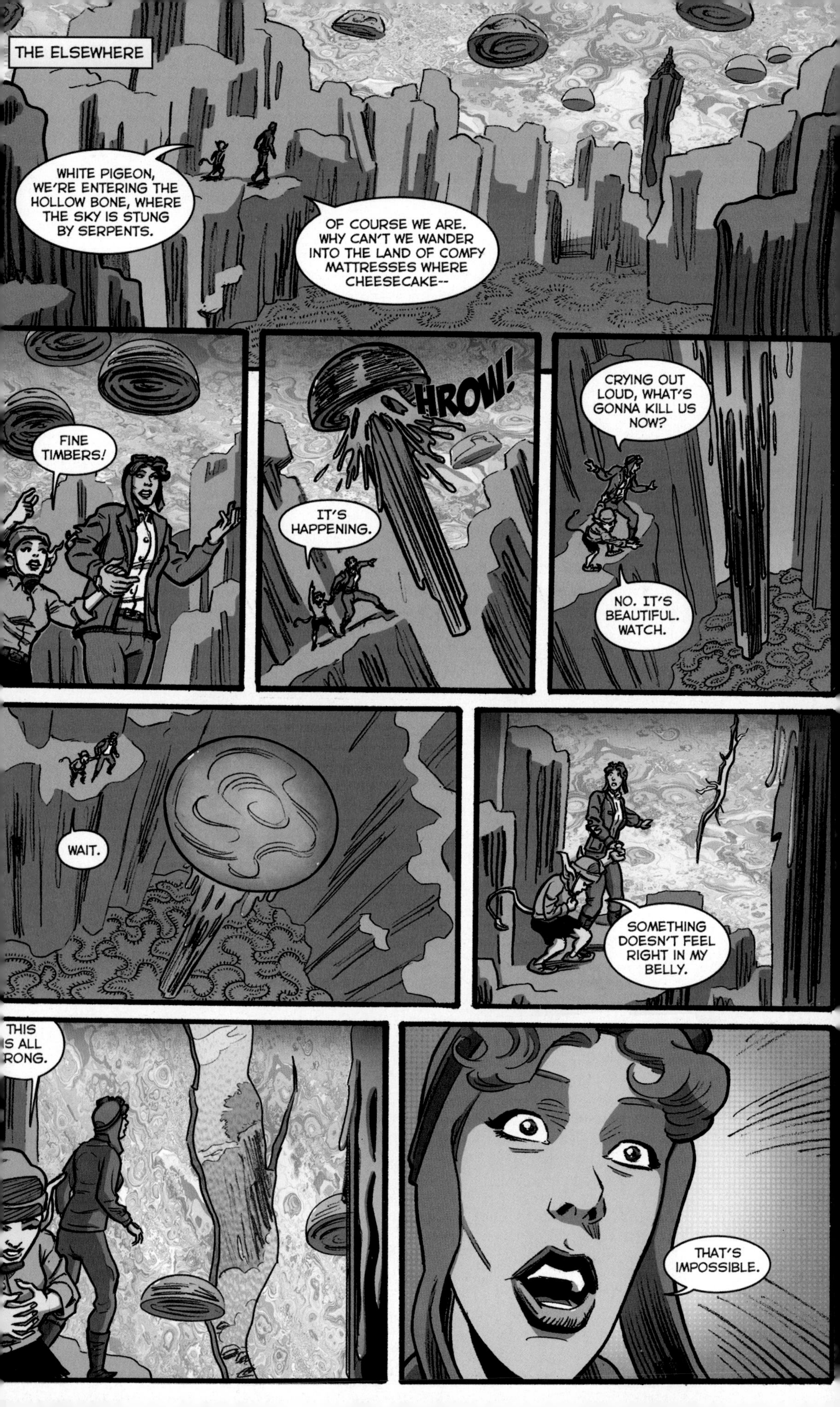

THE ELSEWHERE
WHITE PIGEON, WE'RE ENTERING THE HOLLOW BONE, WHERE THE SKY IS STUNG BY SERPENTS.
OF COURSE WE ARE. WHY CAN'T WE WANDER INTO THE LAND OF COMFY MATTRESSES WHERE CHEESECAKE--
FINE TIMBERS!
HROW!
IT'S HAPPENING.
CRYING OUT LOUD, WHAT'S GONNA KILL US NOW?
NO. IT'S BEAUTIFUL. WATCH.
WAIT.
SOMETHING DOESN'T FEEL RIGHT IN MY BELLY.
THIS
S ALL
RONG.
THAT'S IMPOSSIBLE.

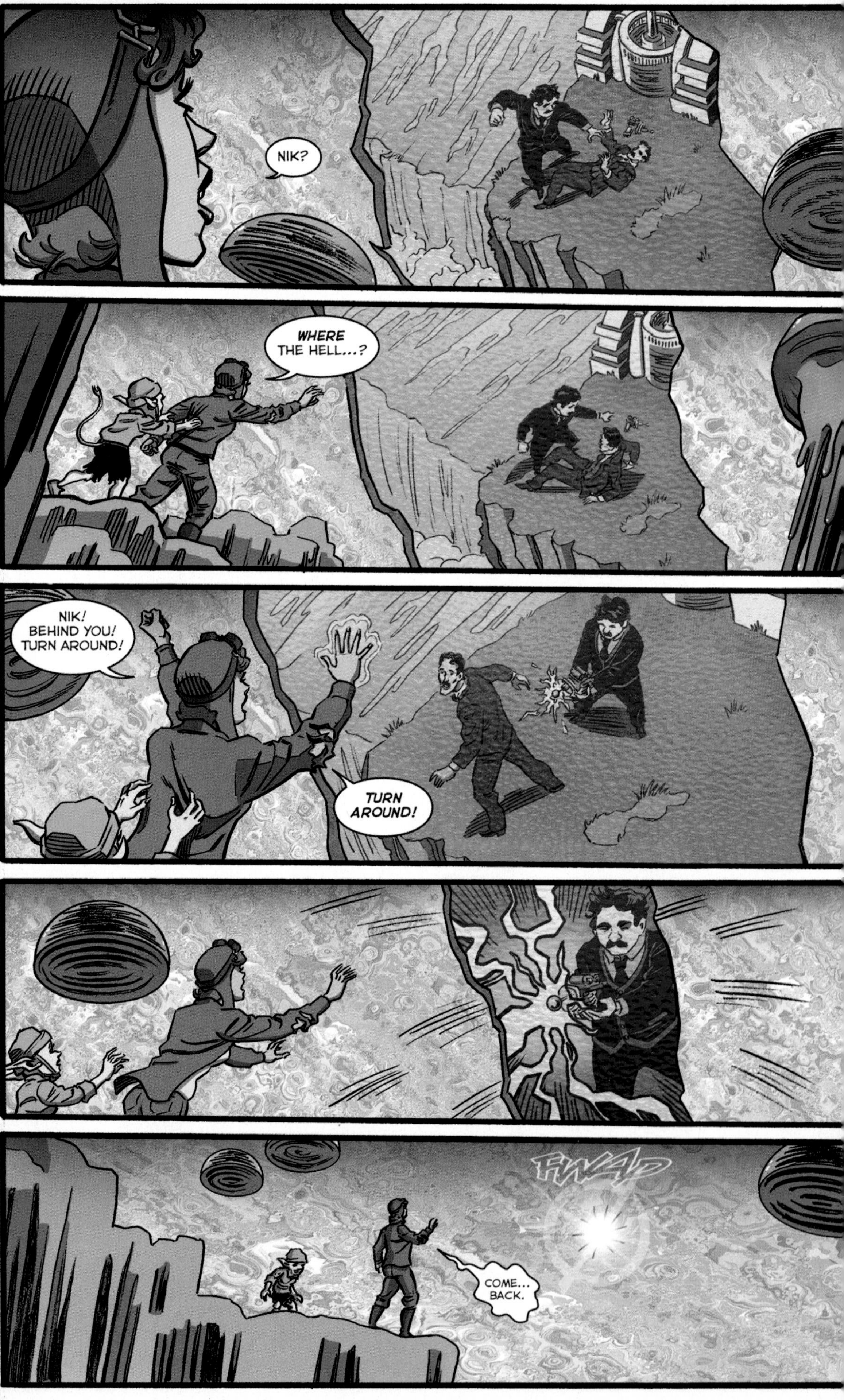
NIK?
WHERE THE HELL...?
NIK! BEHIND YOU! TURN AROUND!
TURN AROUND!
FWAP
COME... BACK.

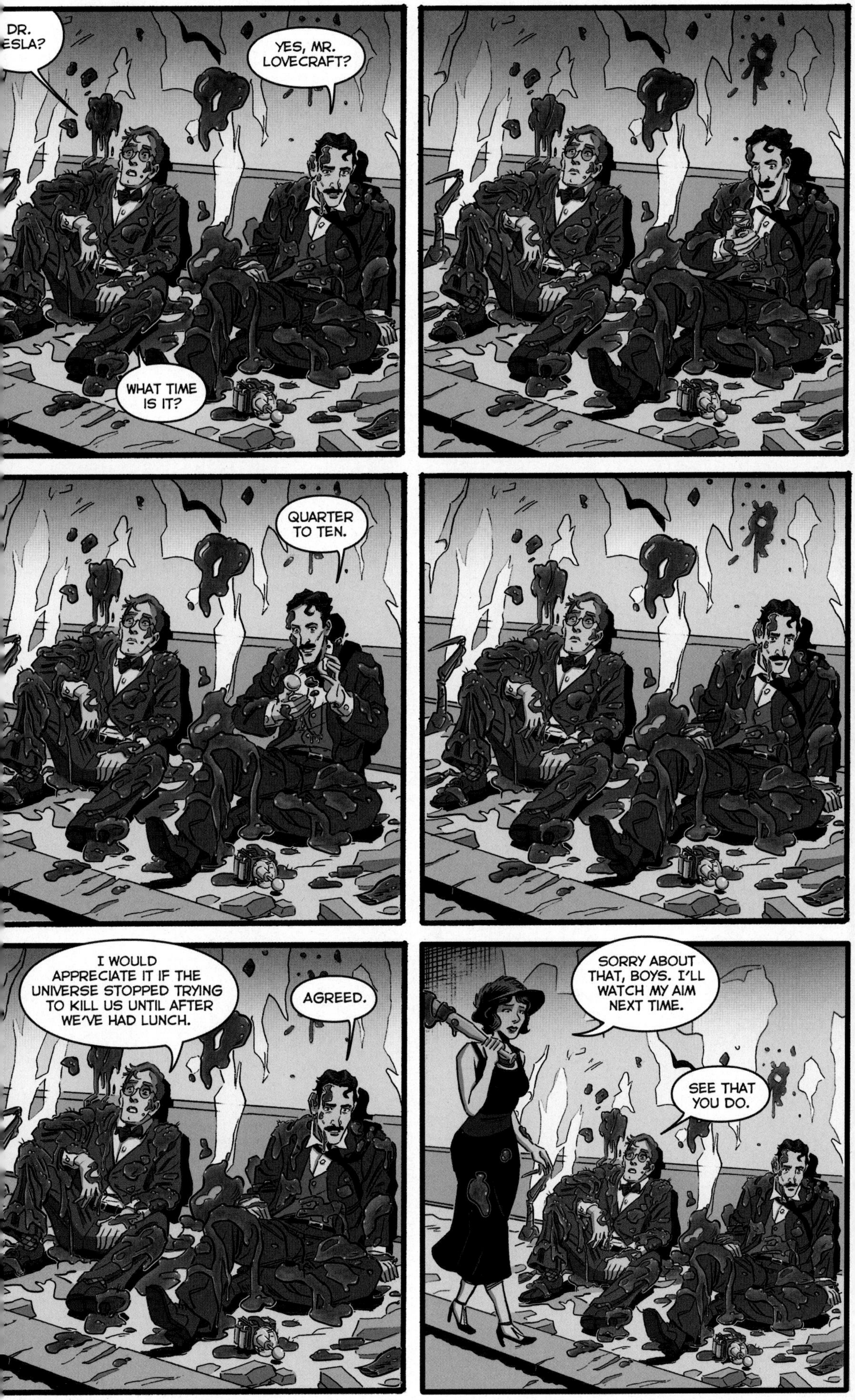
DR. ESLA?
YES, MR. LOVECRAFT?
WHAT TIME IS IT?
QUARTER TO TEN.
I WOULD APPRECIATE IT IF THE UNIVERSE STOPPED TRYING TO KILL US UNTIL AFTER WE'VE HAD LUNCH.
AGREED.
SORRY ABOUT THAT, BOYS. I'LL WATCH MY AIM NEXT TIME.
SEE THAT YOU DO.

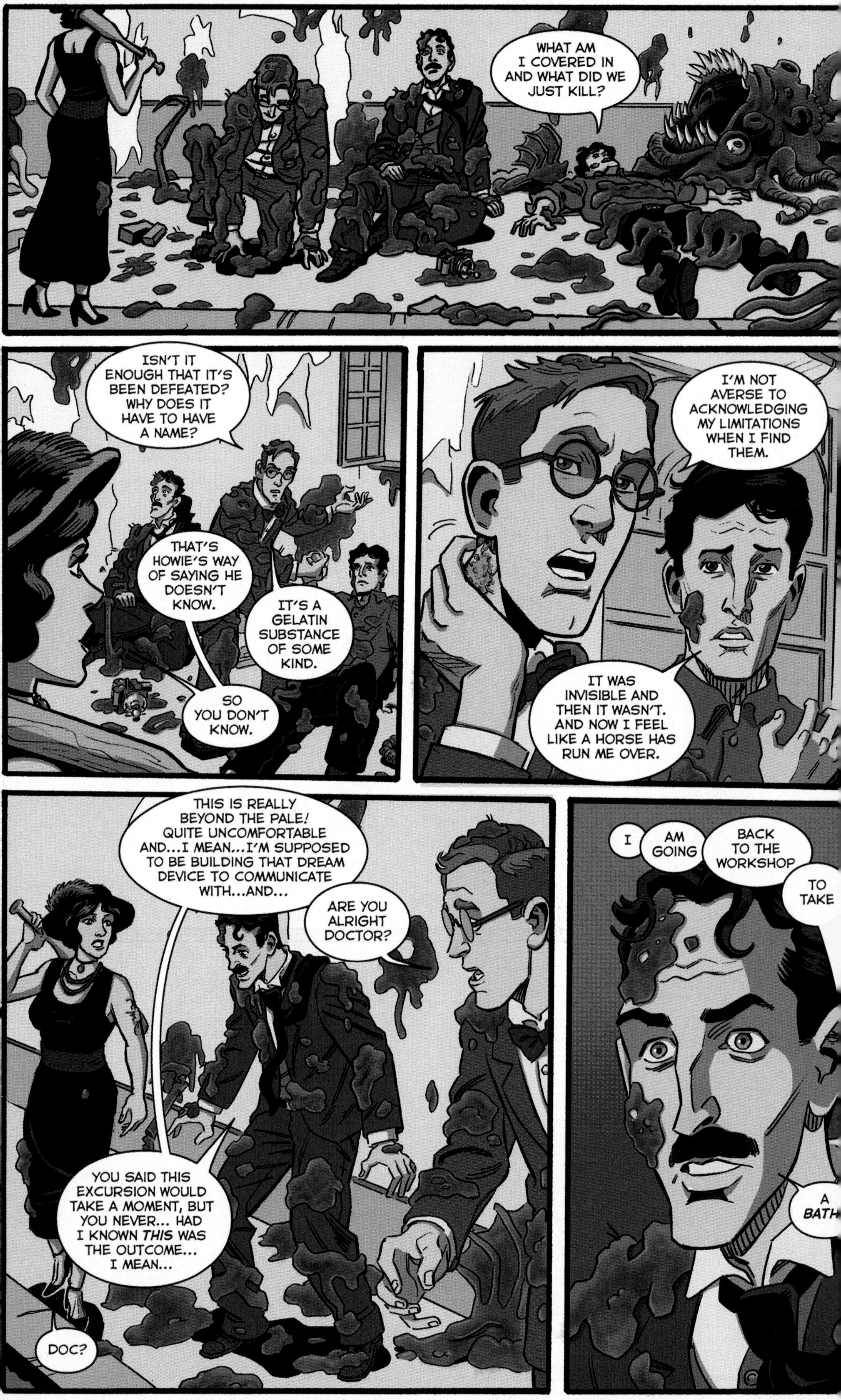
WHAT AM I COVERED IN AND WHAT DID WE JUST KILL?
ISN'T IT ENOUGH THAT IT'S BEEN DEFEATED? WHY DOES IT HAVE TO HAVE A NAME?
THAT'S HOWIE'S WAY OF SAYING HE DOESN'T KNOW.
IT'S A GELATIN SUBSTANCE OF SOME KIND.
SO YOU DON'T KNOW.
I'M NOT AVERSE TO ACKNOWLEDGING MY LIMITATIONS WHEN I FIND THEM.
IT WAS INVISIBLE AND THEN IT WASN'T. AND NOW I FEEL LIKE A HORSE HAS RUN ME OVER.
THIS IS REALLY BEYOND THE PALE! QUITE UNCOMFORTABLE AND...I MEAN...I'M SUPPOSED TO BE BUILDING THAT DREAM DEVICE TO COMMUNICATE WITH...AND...
ARE YOU ALRIGHT DOCTOR?
YOU SAID THIS EXCURSION WOULD TAKE A MOMENT, BUT YOU NEVER... HAD I KNOWN *THIS* WAS THE OUTCOME... I MEAN...
DOC?
I
AM GOING
BACK TO THE WORKSHOP
TO TAKE
A *BATH*

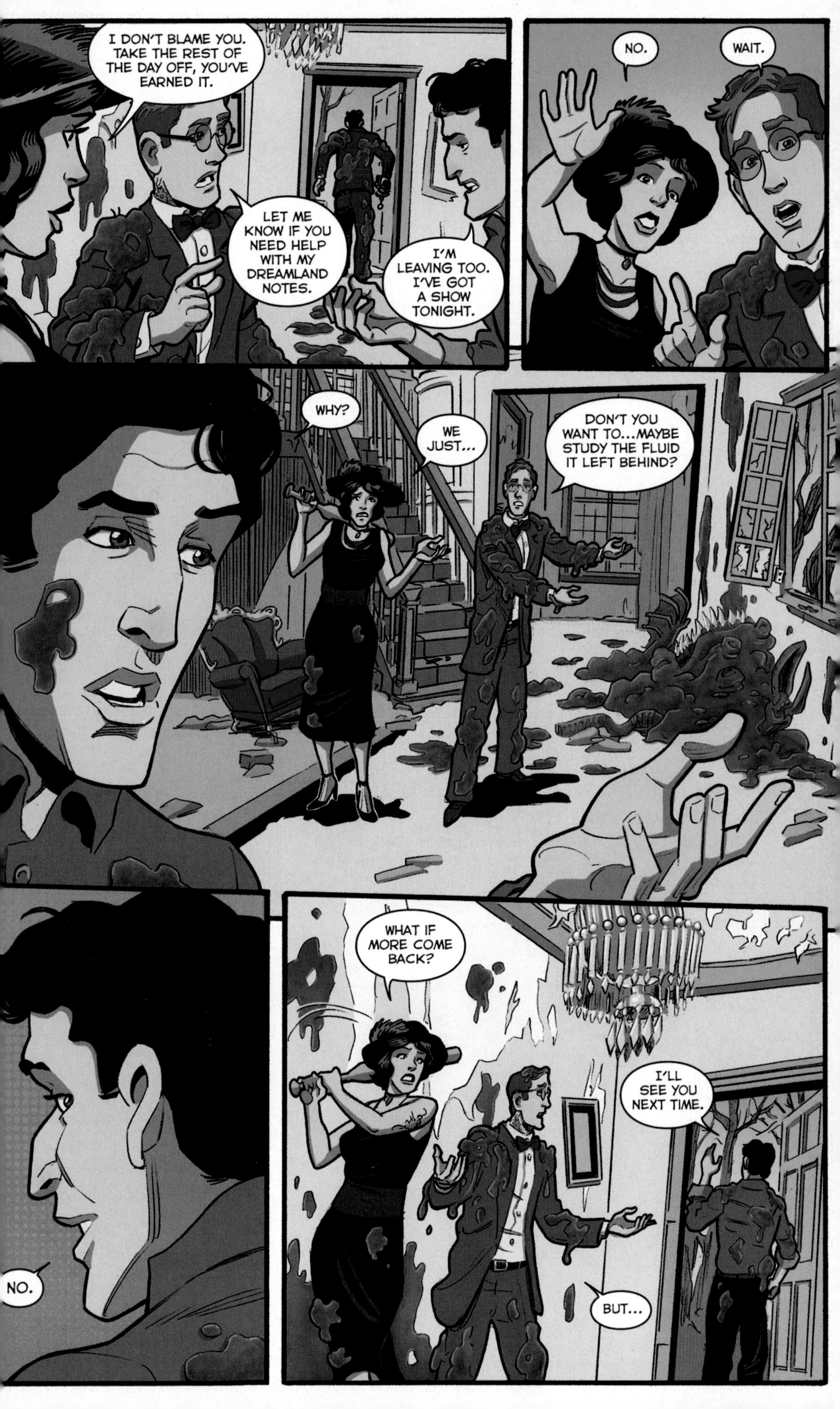
I DON'T BLAME YOU. TAKE THE REST OF THE DAY OFF, YOU'VE EARNED IT.
LET ME KNOW IF YOU NEED HELP WITH MY DREAMLAND NOTES.
I'M LEAVING TOO. I'VE GOT A SHOW TONIGHT.
NO.
WAIT.
WHY?
WE JUST...
DON'T YOU WANT TO...MAYBE STUDY THE FLUID IT LEFT BEHIND?
NO.
WHAT IF MORE COME BACK?
I'LL SEE YOU NEXT TIME.
BUT...

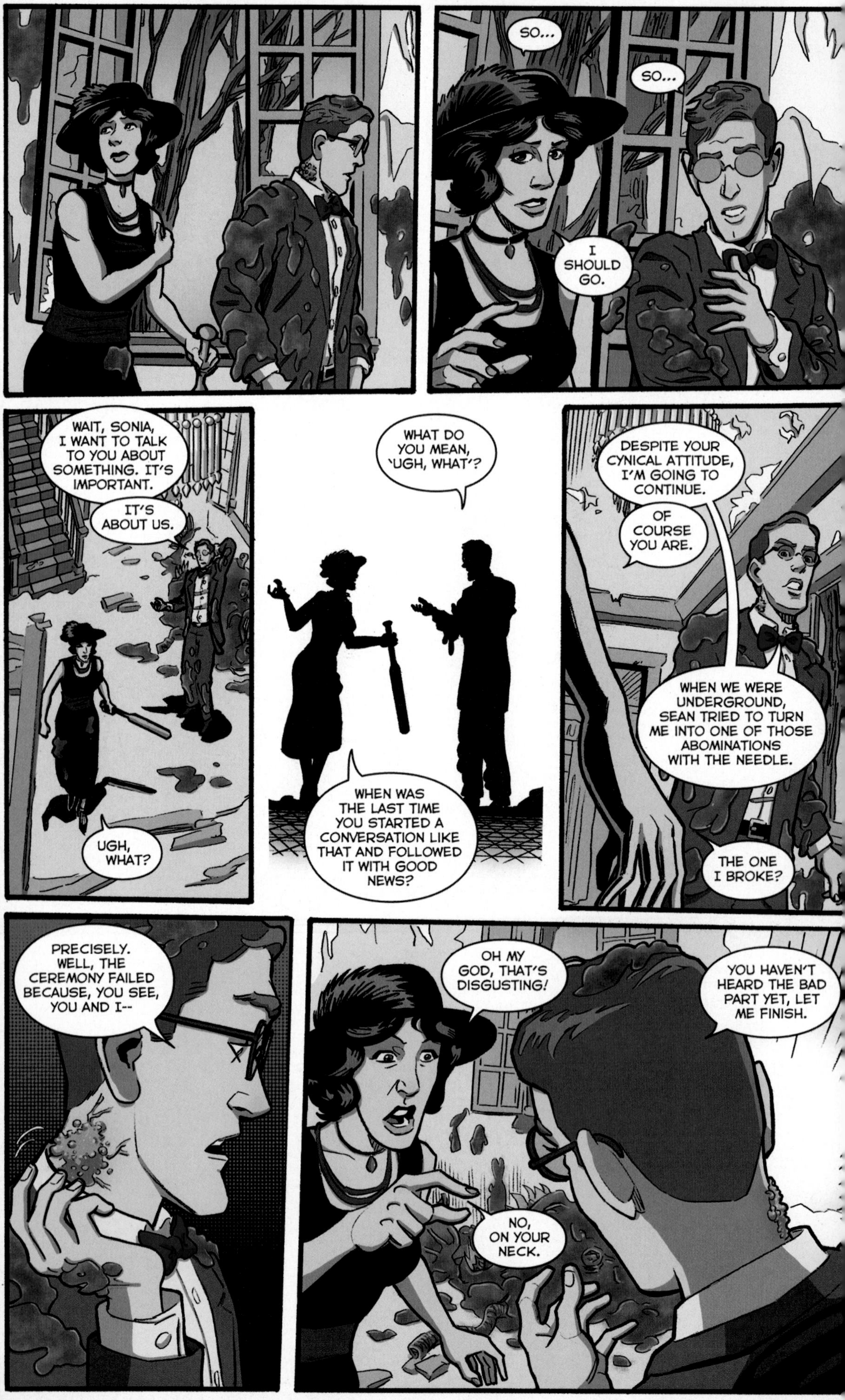
SO...
SO...
I SHOULD GO.
WAIT, SONIA, I WANT TO TALK TO YOU ABOUT SOMETHING. IT'S IMPORTANT.
IT'S ABOUT US.
UGH, WHAT?
WHAT DO YOU MEAN, 'UGH, WHAT'?
WHEN WAS THE LAST TIME YOU STARTED A CONVERSATION LIKE THAT AND FOLLOWED IT WITH GOOD NEWS?
DESPITE YOUR CYNICAL ATTITUDE, I'M GOING TO CONTINUE.
OF COURSE YOU ARE.
WHEN WE WERE UNDERGROUND, SEAN TRIED TO TURN ME INTO ONE OF THOSE ABOMINATIONS WITH THE NEEDLE.
THE ONE I BROKE?
PRECISELY. WELL, THE CEREMONY FAILED BECAUSE, YOU SEE, YOU AND I--
OH MY GOD, THAT'S DISGUSTING!
YOU HAVEN'T HEARD THE BAD PART YET, LET ME FINISH.
NO, ON YOUR NECK.

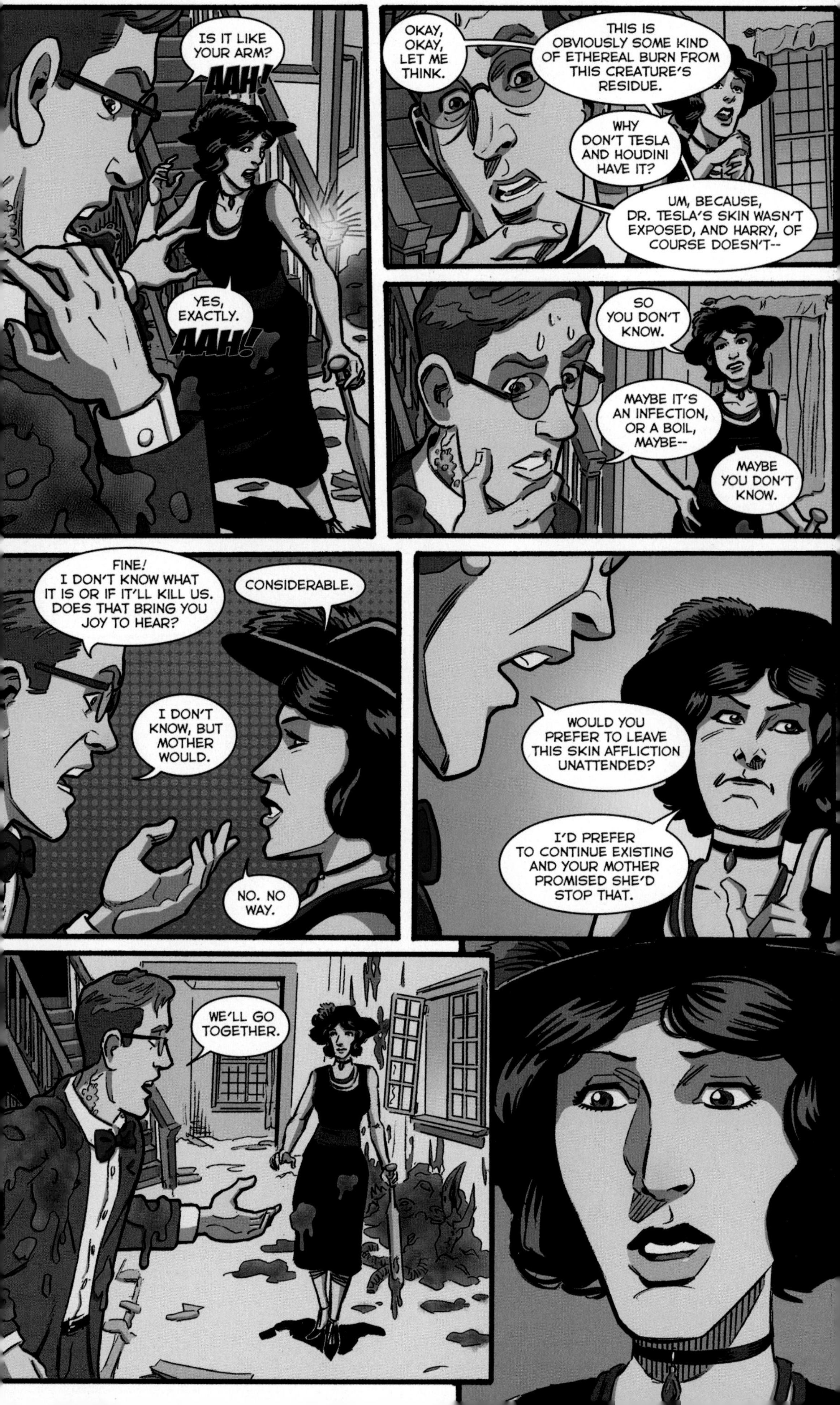
IS IT LIKE YOUR ARM?
AAH!
YES, EXACTLY.
AAH!
OKAY, OKAY, LET ME THINK.
THIS IS OBVIOUSLY SOME KIND OF ETHEREAL BURN FROM THIS CREATURE'S RESIDUE.
WHY DON'T TESLA AND HOUDINI HAVE IT?
UM, BECAUSE, DR. TESLA'S SKIN WASN'T EXPOSED, AND HARRY, OF COURSE DOESN'T--
SO YOU DON'T KNOW.
MAYBE IT'S AN INFECTION, OR A BOIL, MAYBE--
MAYBE YOU DON'T KNOW.
FINE! I DON'T KNOW WHAT IT IS OR IF IT'LL KILL US. DOES THAT BRING YOU JOY TO HEAR?
CONSIDERABLE.
I DON'T KNOW, BUT MOTHER WOULD.
NO. NO WAY.
WOULD YOU PREFER TO LEAVE THIS SKIN AFFLICTION UNATTENDED?
I'D PREFER TO CONTINUE EXISTING AND YOUR MOTHER PROMISED SHE'D STOP THAT.
WE'LL GO TOGETHER.

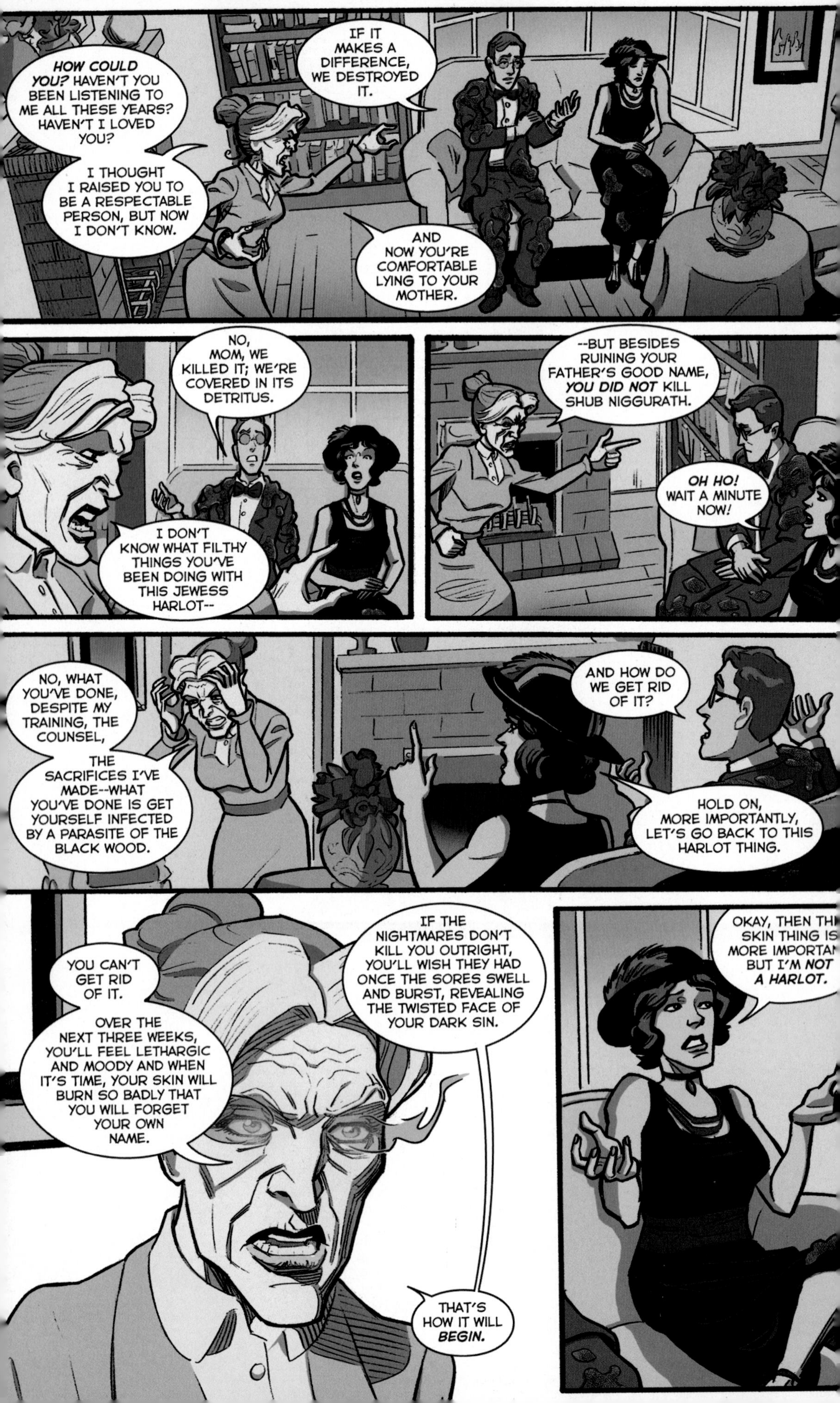

HOW COULD YOU? HAVEN'T YOU BEEN LISTENING TO ME ALL THESE YEARS? HAVEN'T I LOVED YOU?
IF IT MAKES A DIFFERENCE, WE DESTROYED IT.
I THOUGHT I RAISED YOU TO BE A RESPECTABLE PERSON, BUT NOW I DON'T KNOW.
AND NOW YOU'RE COMFORTABLE LYING TO YOUR MOTHER.
NO, MOM, WE KILLED IT; WE'RE COVERED IN ITS DETRITUS.
I DON'T KNOW WHAT FILTHY THINGS YOU'VE BEEN DOING WITH THIS JEWESS HARLOT--
--BUT BESIDES RUINING YOUR FATHER'S GOOD NAME, YOU DID NOT KILL SHUB NIGGURATH.
OH HO! WAIT A MINUTE NOW!
NO, WHAT YOU'VE DONE, DESPITE MY TRAINING, THE COUNSEL,
THE SACRIFICES I'VE MADE--WHAT YOU'VE DONE IS GET YOURSELF INFECTED BY A PARASITE OF THE BLACK WOOD.
AND HOW DO WE GET RID OF IT?
HOLD ON, MORE IMPORTANTLY, LET'S GO BACK TO THIS HARLOT THING.
YOU CAN'T GET RID OF IT.
OVER THE NEXT THREE WEEKS, YOU'LL FEEL LETHARGIC AND MOODY AND WHEN IT'S TIME, YOUR SKIN WILL BURN SO BADLY THAT YOU WILL FORGET YOUR OWN NAME.
IF THE NIGHTMARES DON'T KILL YOU OUTRIGHT, YOU'LL WISH THEY HAD ONCE THE SORES SWELL AND BURST, REVEALING THE TWISTED FACE OF YOUR DARK SIN.
THAT'S HOW IT WILL BEGIN.
OKAY, THEN TH SKIN THING IS MORE IMPORTAN BUT I'M NOT A HARLOT.

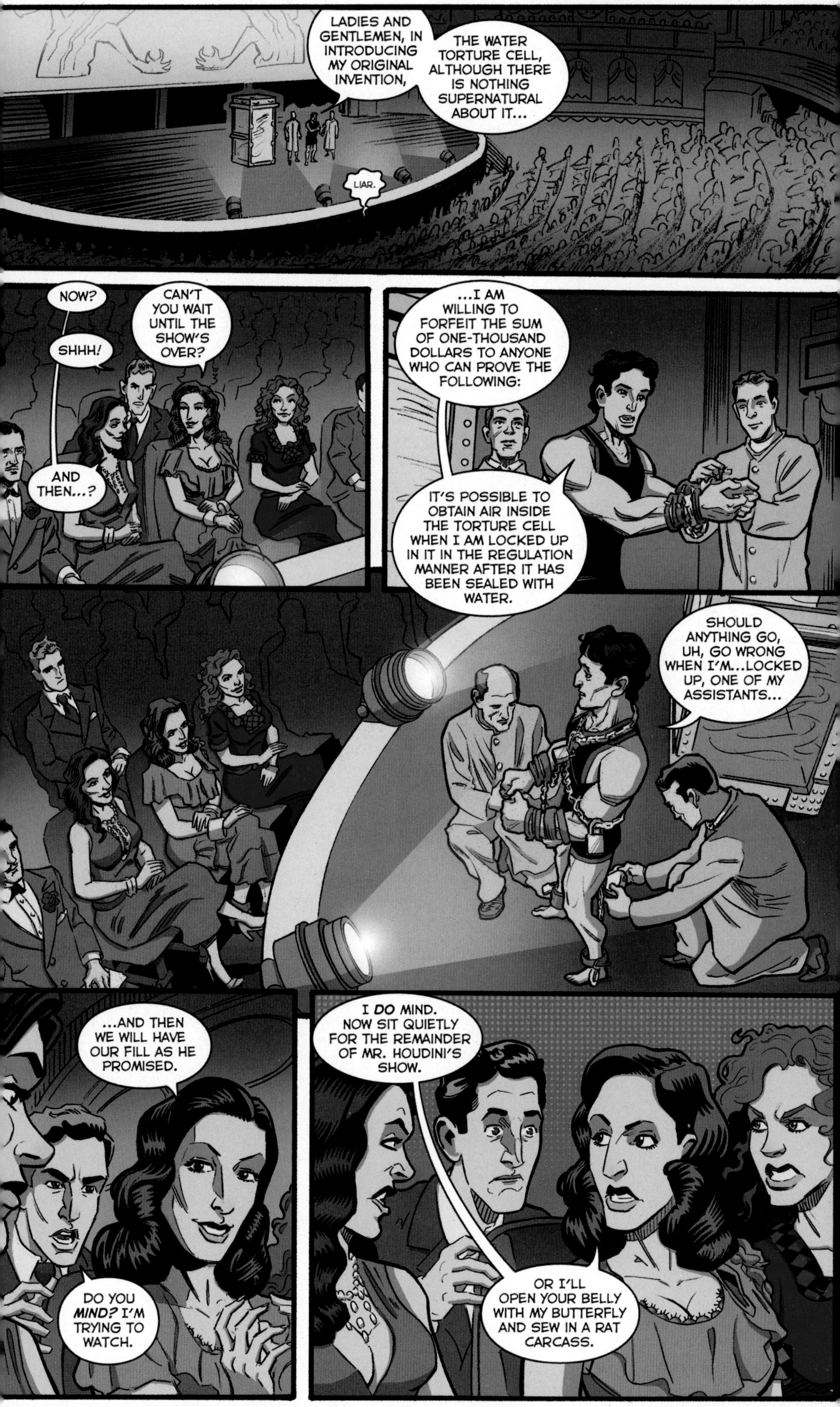
LADIES AND GENTLEMEN, IN INTRODUCING MY ORIGINAL INVENTION,
THE WATER TORTURE CELL, ALTHOUGH THERE IS NOTHING SUPERNATURAL ABOUT IT...
LIAR.
NOW?
SHHH!
CAN'T YOU WAIT UNTIL THE SHOW'S OVER?
AND THEN...?
...I AM WILLING TO FORFEIT THE SUM OF ONE-THOUSAND DOLLARS TO ANYONE WHO CAN PROVE THE FOLLOWING:
IT'S POSSIBLE TO OBTAIN AIR INSIDE THE TORTURE CELL WHEN I AM LOCKED UP IN IT IN THE REGULATION MANNER AFTER IT HAS BEEN SEALED WITH WATER.
SHOULD ANYTHING GO, UH, GO WRONG WHEN I'M...LOCKED UP, ONE OF MY ASSISTANTS...
...AND THEN WE WILL HAVE OUR FILL AS HE PROMISED.
DO YOU *MIND?* I'M TRYING TO WATCH.
I *DO* MIND. NOW SIT QUIETLY FOR THE REMAINDER OF MR. HOUDINI'S SHOW.
OR I'LL OPEN YOUR BELLY WITH MY BUTTERFLY AND SEW IN A RAT CARCASS.

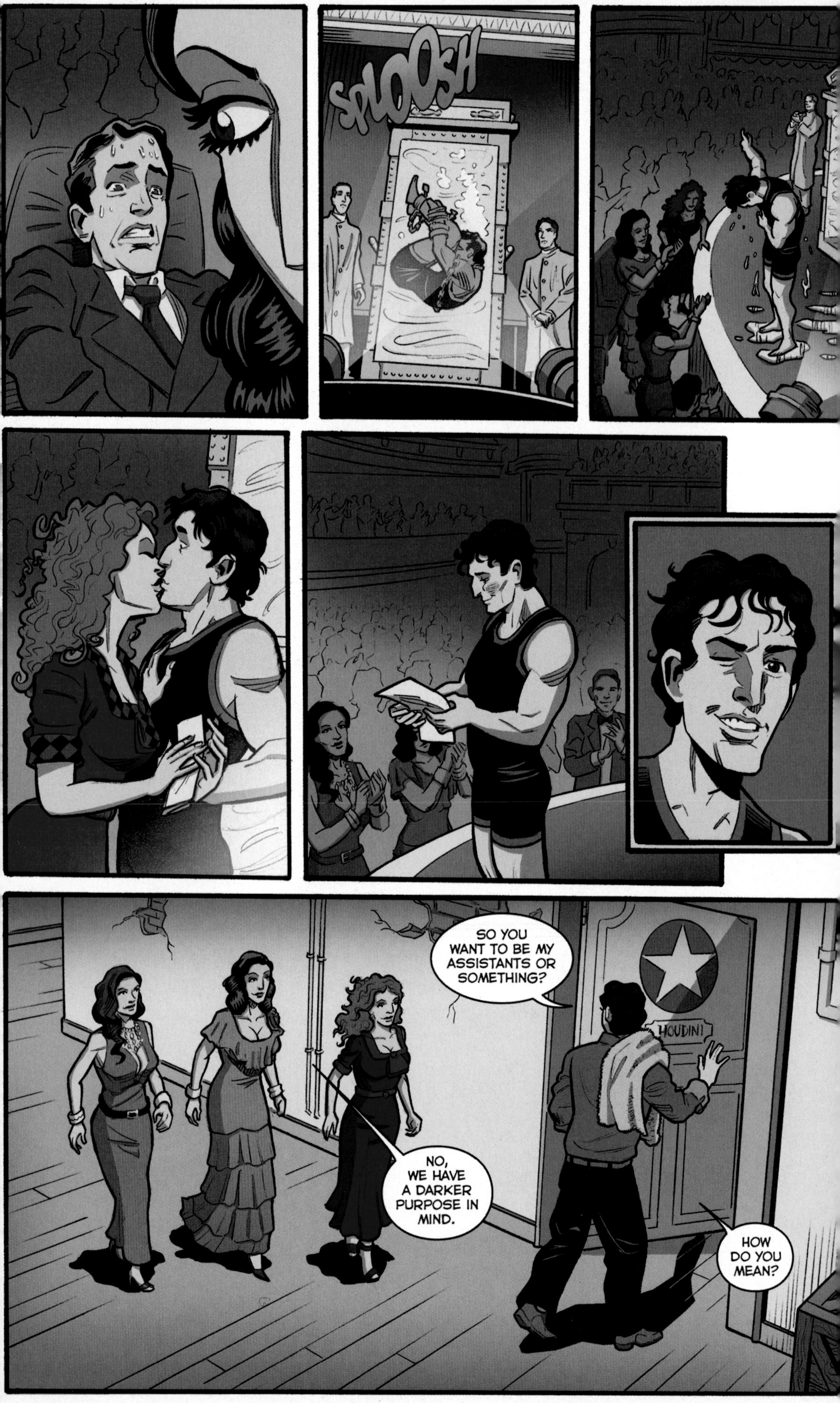
SPLOOSH
SO YOU WANT TO BE MY ASSISTANTS OR SOMETHING?
HOUDINI
NO, WE HAVE A DARKER PURPOSE IN MIND.
HOW DO YOU MEAN?

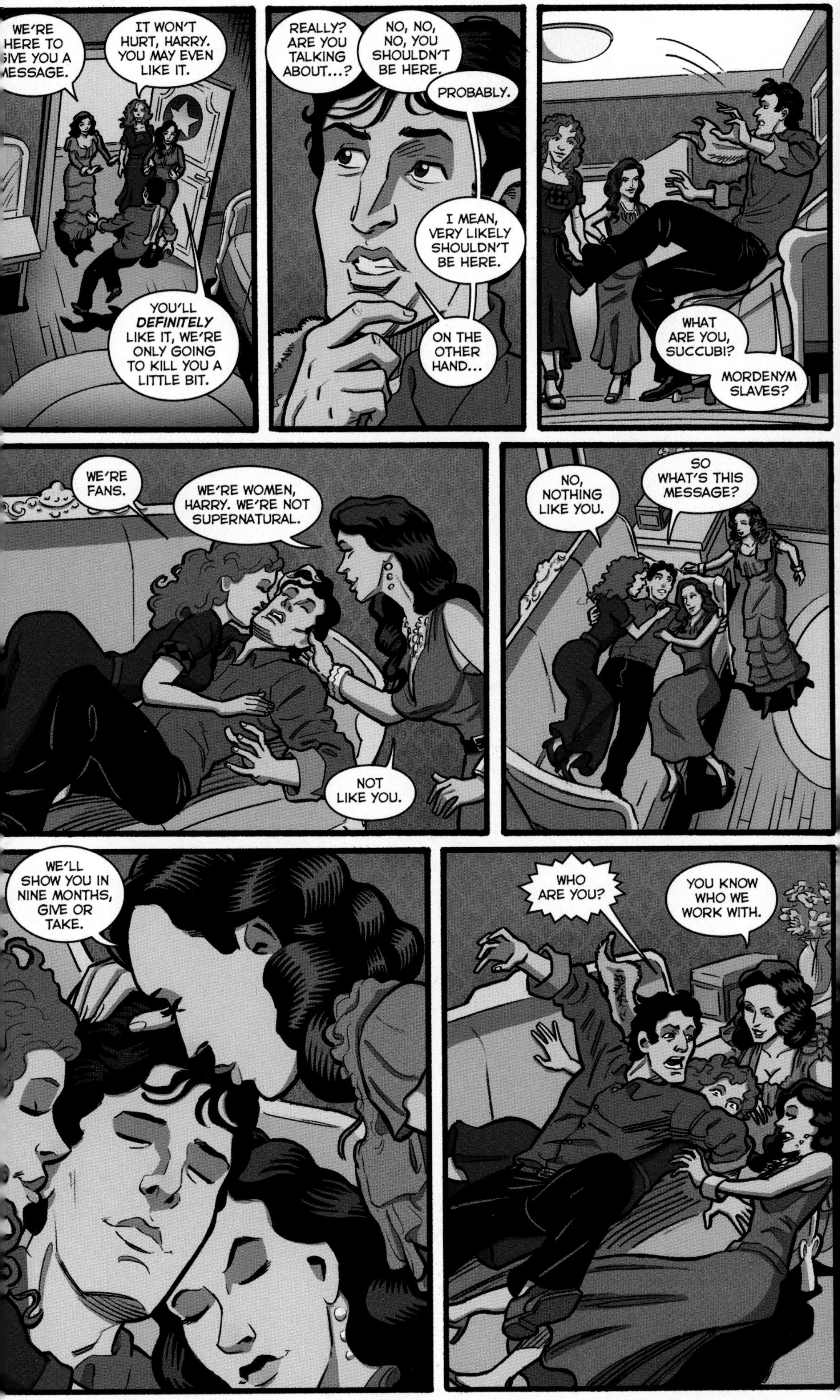
WE'RE HERE TO GIVE YOU A MESSAGE.
IT WON'T HURT, HARRY. YOU MAY EVEN LIKE IT.
YOU'LL *DEFINITELY* LIKE IT, WE'RE ONLY GOING TO KILL YOU A LITTLE BIT.
REALLY? ARE YOU TALKING ABOUT...?
NO, NO, NO, YOU SHOULDN'T BE HERE.
PROBABLY.
I MEAN, VERY LIKELY SHOULDN'T BE HERE.
ON THE OTHER HAND...
WHAT ARE YOU, SUCCUBI?
MORDENYM SLAVES?
WE'RE FANS.
WE'RE WOMEN, HARRY. WE'RE NOT SUPERNATURAL.
NOT LIKE YOU.
NO, NOTHING LIKE YOU.
SO WHAT'S THIS MESSAGE?
WE'LL SHOW YOU IN NINE MONTHS, GIVE OR TAKE.
WHO ARE YOU?
YOU KNOW WHO WE WORK WITH.

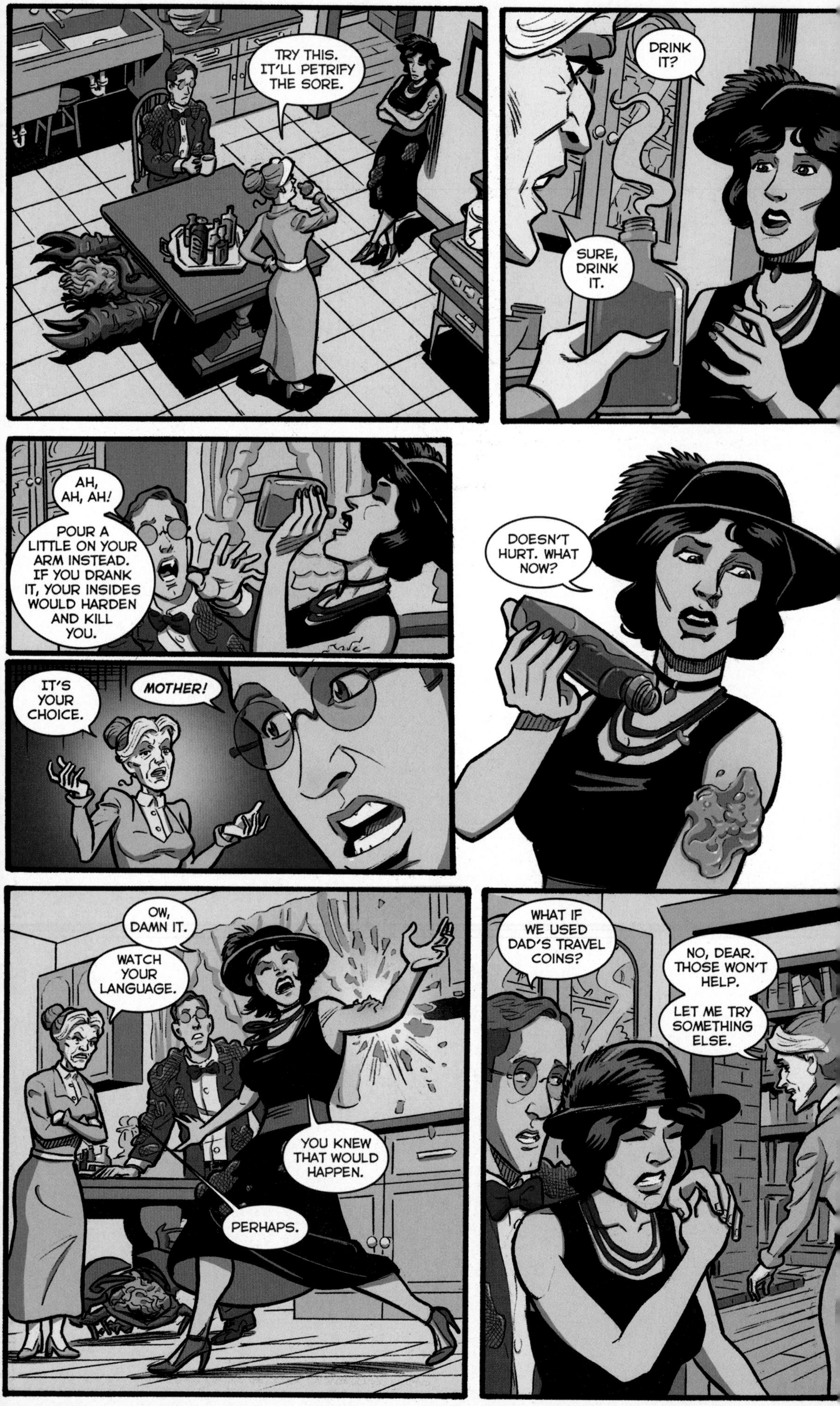
TRY THIS. IT'LL PETRIFY THE SORE.
DRINK IT?
SURE, DRINK IT.
AH, AH, AH!
POUR A LITTLE ON YOUR ARM INSTEAD. IF YOU DRANK IT, YOUR INSIDES WOULD HARDEN AND KILL YOU.
IT'S YOUR CHOICE.
MOTHER!
DOESN'T HURT. WHAT NOW?
OW, DAMN IT.
WATCH YOUR LANGUAGE.
YOU KNEW THAT WOULD HAPPEN.
PERHAPS.
WHAT IF WE USED DAD'S TRAVEL COINS?
NO, DEAR. THOSE WON'T HELP.
LET ME TRY SOMETHING ELSE.

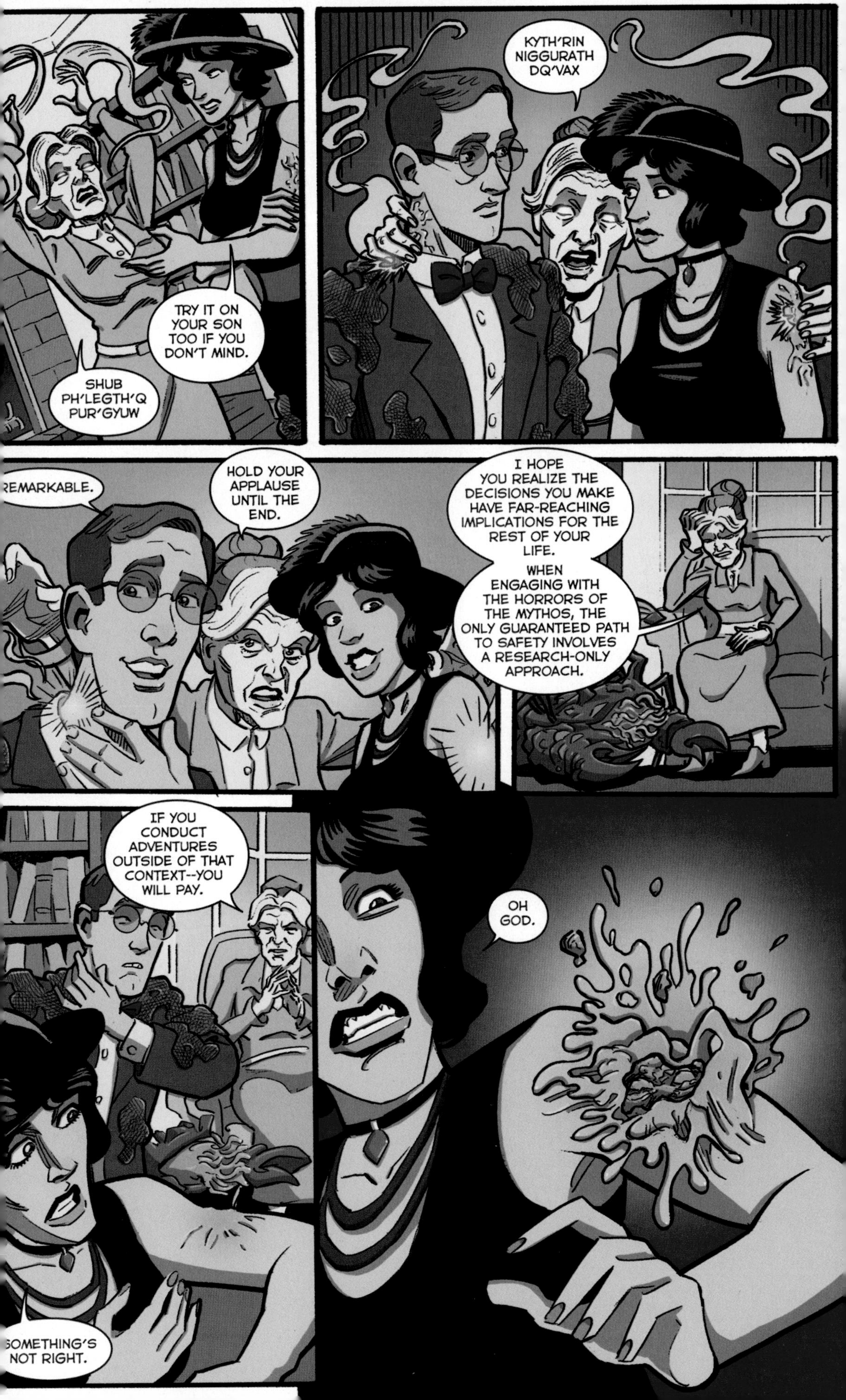
TRY IT ON YOUR SON TOO IF YOU DON'T MIND.
SHUB PH'LEGTH'Q PUR'GYUW
KYTH'RIN NIGGURATH DQ'VAX
REMARKABLE.
HOLD YOUR APPLAUSE UNTIL THE END.
I HOPE YOU REALIZE THE DECISIONS YOU MAKE HAVE FAR-REACHING IMPLICATIONS FOR THE REST OF YOUR LIFE.
WHEN ENGAGING WITH THE HORRORS OF THE MYTHOS, THE ONLY GUARANTEED PATH TO SAFETY INVOLVES A RESEARCH-ONLY APPROACH.
IF YOU CONDUCT ADVENTURES OUTSIDE OF THAT CONTEXT--YOU WILL PAY.
SOMETHING'S NOT RIGHT.
OH GOD.

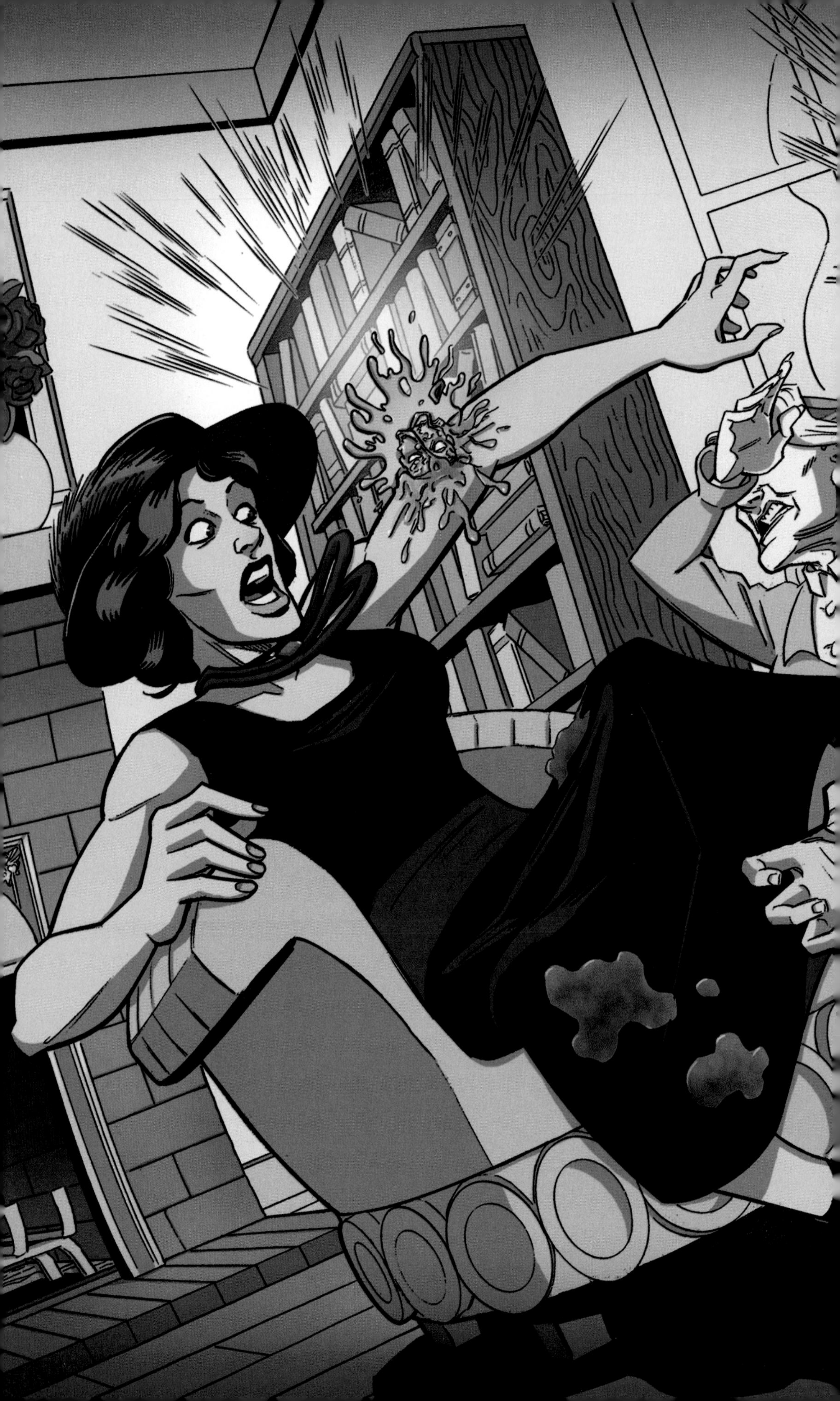

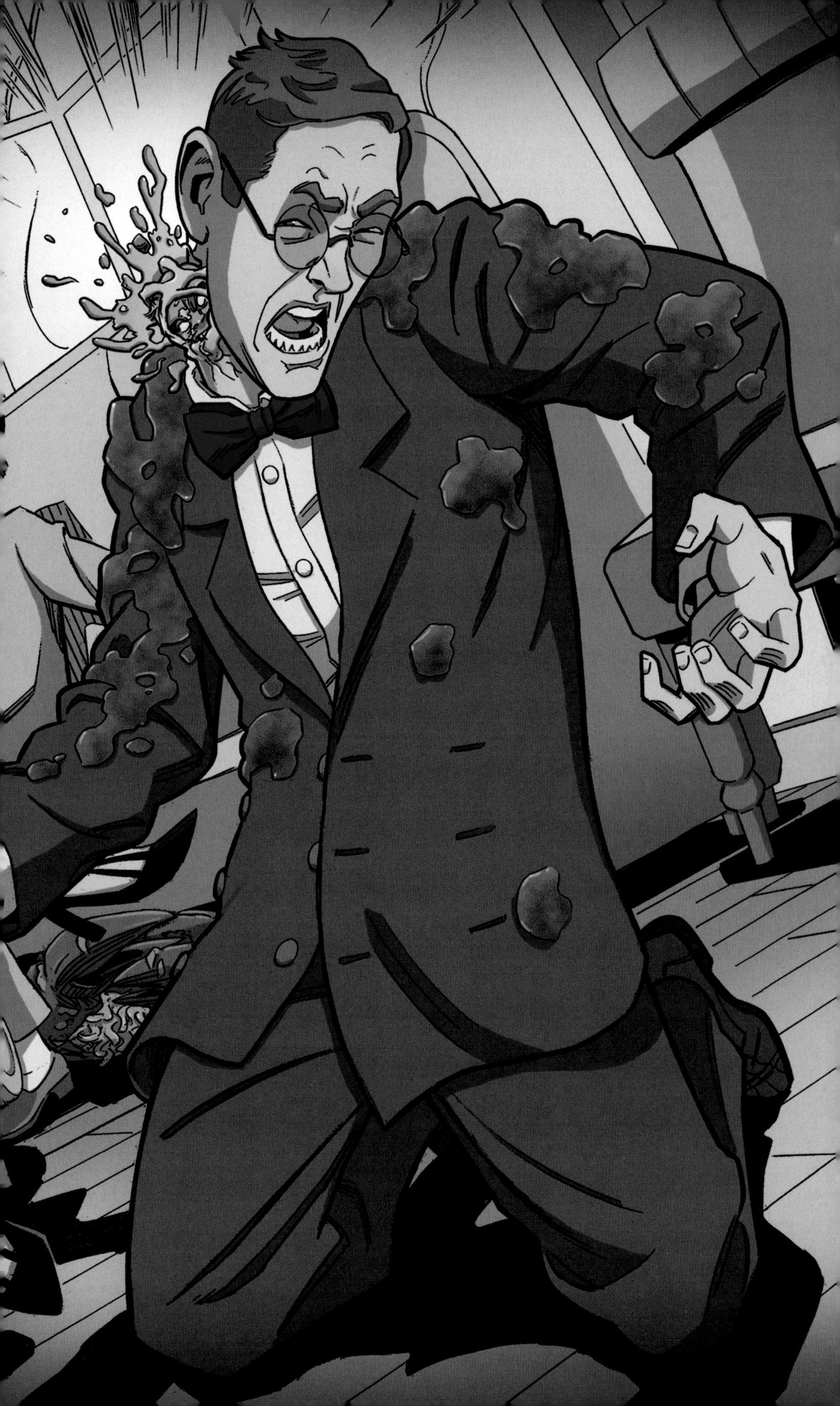

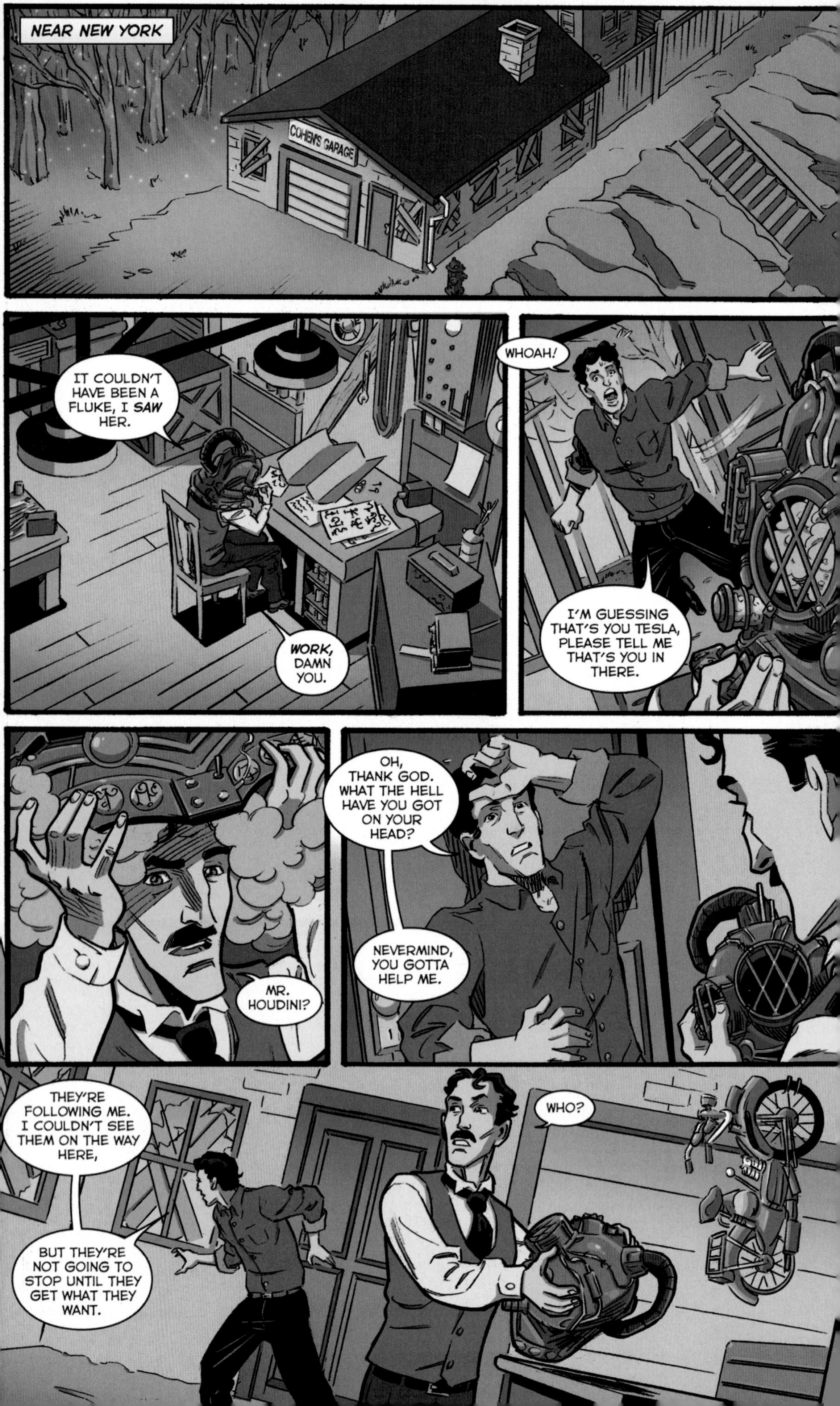
NEAR NEW YORK
COHEN'S GARAGE
IT COULDN'T HAVE BEEN A FLUKE, I SAW HER.
WORK, DAMN YOU.
WHOAH!
I'M GUESSING THAT'S YOU TESLA, PLEASE TELL ME THAT'S YOU IN THERE.
MR. HOUDINI?
OH, THANK GOD. WHAT THE HELL HAVE YOU GOT ON YOUR HEAD?
NEVERMIND, YOU GOTTA HELP ME.
THEY'RE FOLLOWING ME. I COULDN'T SEE THEM ON THE WAY HERE,
BUT THEY'RE NOT GOING TO STOP UNTIL THEY GET WHAT THEY WANT.
WHO?

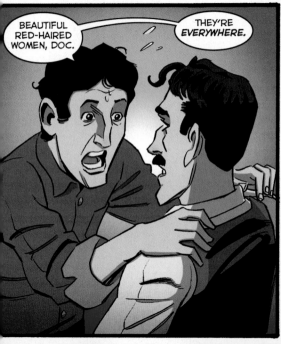

BEAUTIFUL RED-HAIRED WOMEN, DOC.

THEY'RE *EVERYWHERE.*

HAVE A SEAT AND TAKE A DEEP BREATH, MR. HOUDINI. I'M GOING TO PUT THIS ON YOUR HEAD AND SEE WHAT HAPPENS.

YEAH, OKAY.

WAIT, WAIT A MINUTE, THEY'RE COMING, YOU'VE GOT TO SAVE ME.

FROM YOUR ADORING FANS? I THINK YOU'LL SURVIVE.

NOW BE STILL. YOUR INSTINCT WILL BE TO SHUT YOUR EYES, BUT DO YOUR BEST TO KEEP THEM OPEN.

WHAT IS THIS THING?

THIS IS THE CERYX EX PRAETERITO. I'VE BEEN DEVELOPING IT WITH MR. LOVECRAFT AT THE BEHEST OF MR. TWAIN. IT'S DESIGNED TO MAKE CONTACT WITH THE DREAMLANDS,

BUT SO FAR IT'S BEEN SPOTTY AT BEST. I WANT YOU TO TELL ME WHAT YOU SEE.

I DON'T SEE ANYTHING.

WAIT...

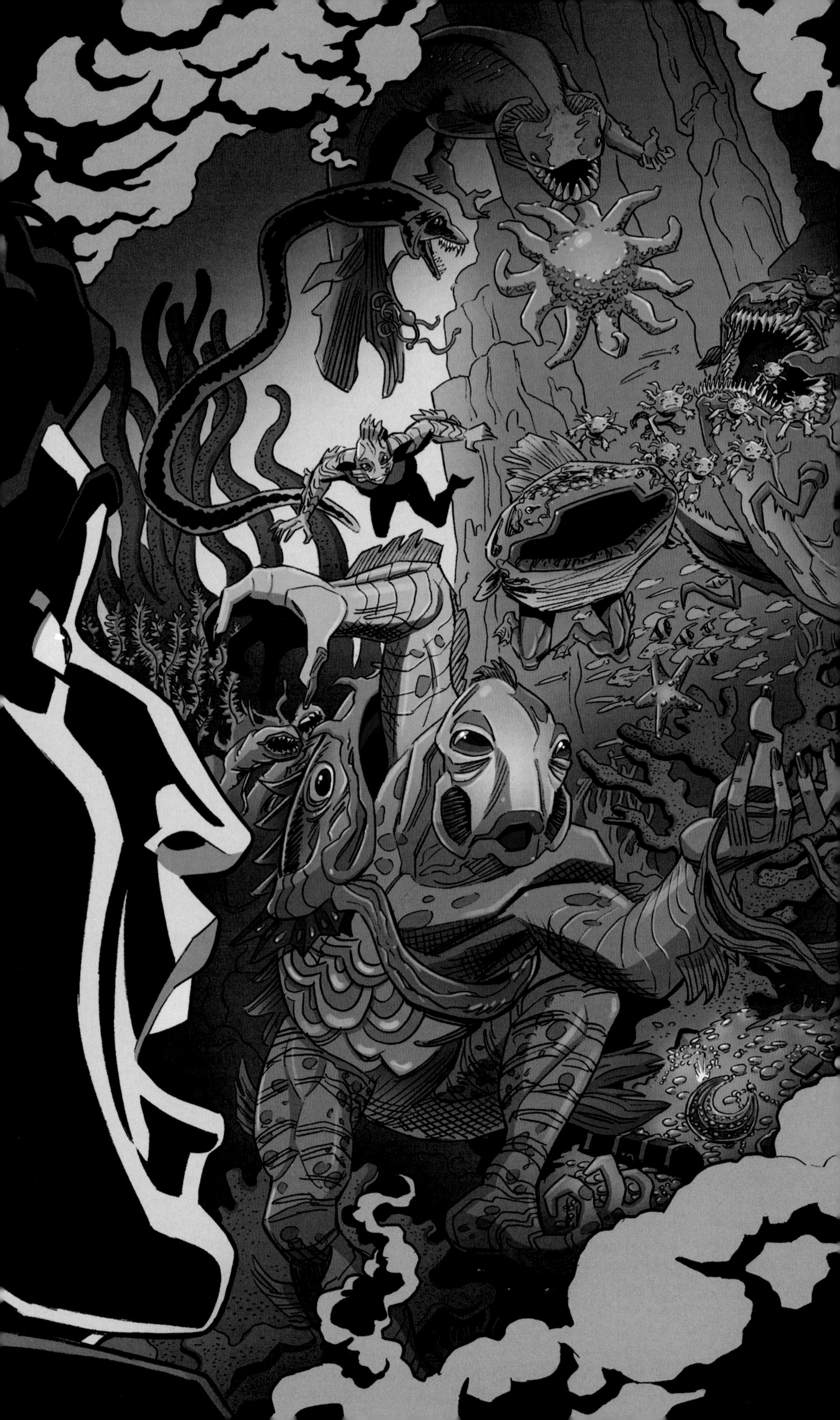

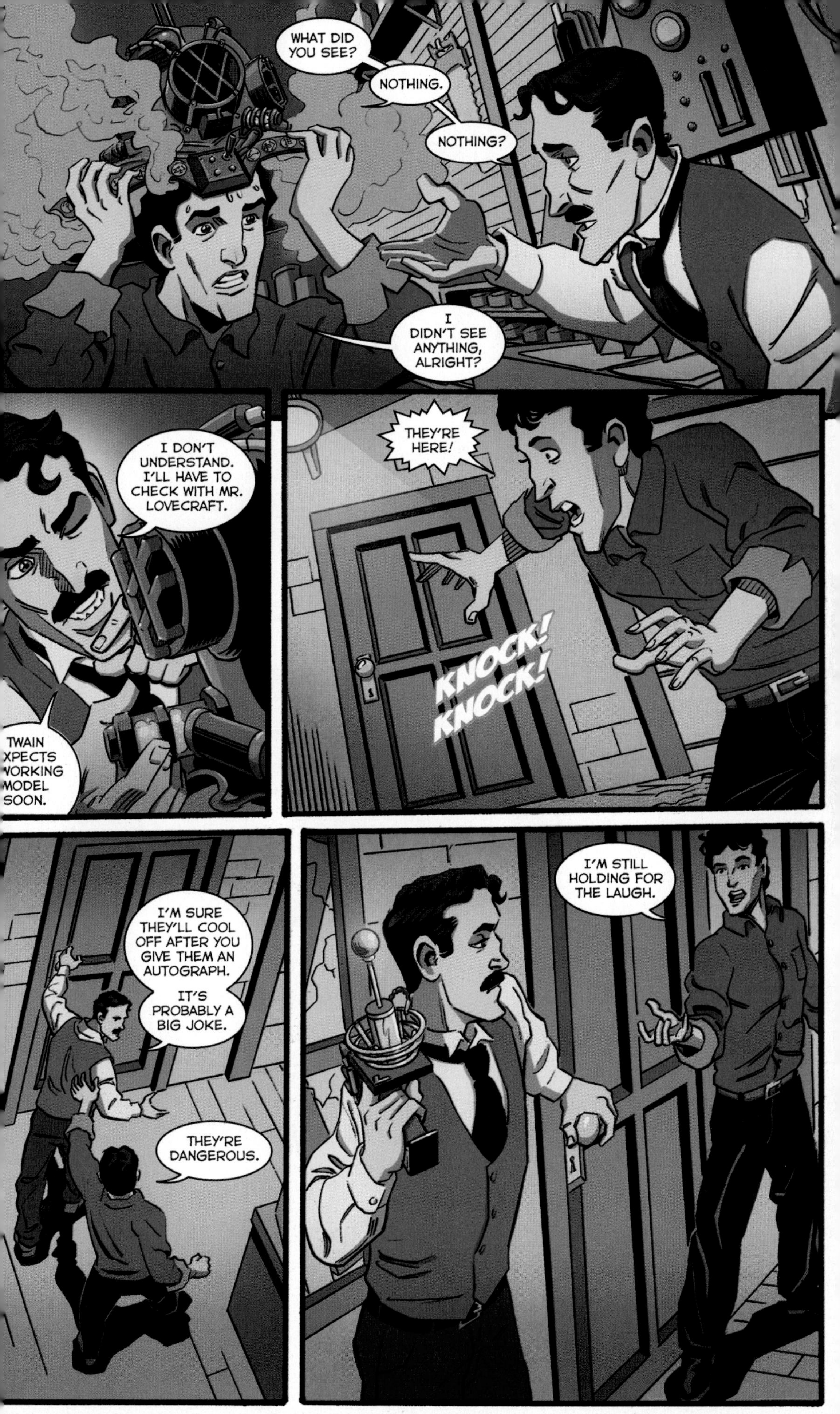
WHAT DID YOU SEE?
NOTHING.
NOTHING?
I DIDN'T SEE ANYTHING, ALRIGHT?
I DON'T UNDERSTAND. I'LL HAVE TO CHECK WITH MR. LOVECRAFT.
TWAIN XPECTS WORKING MODEL SOON.
THEY'RE HERE!
KNOCK! KNOCK!
I'M SURE THEY'LL COOL OFF AFTER YOU GIVE THEM AN AUTOGRAPH.
IT'S PROBABLY A BIG JOKE.
THEY'RE DANGEROUS.
I'M STILL HOLDING FOR THE LAUGH.

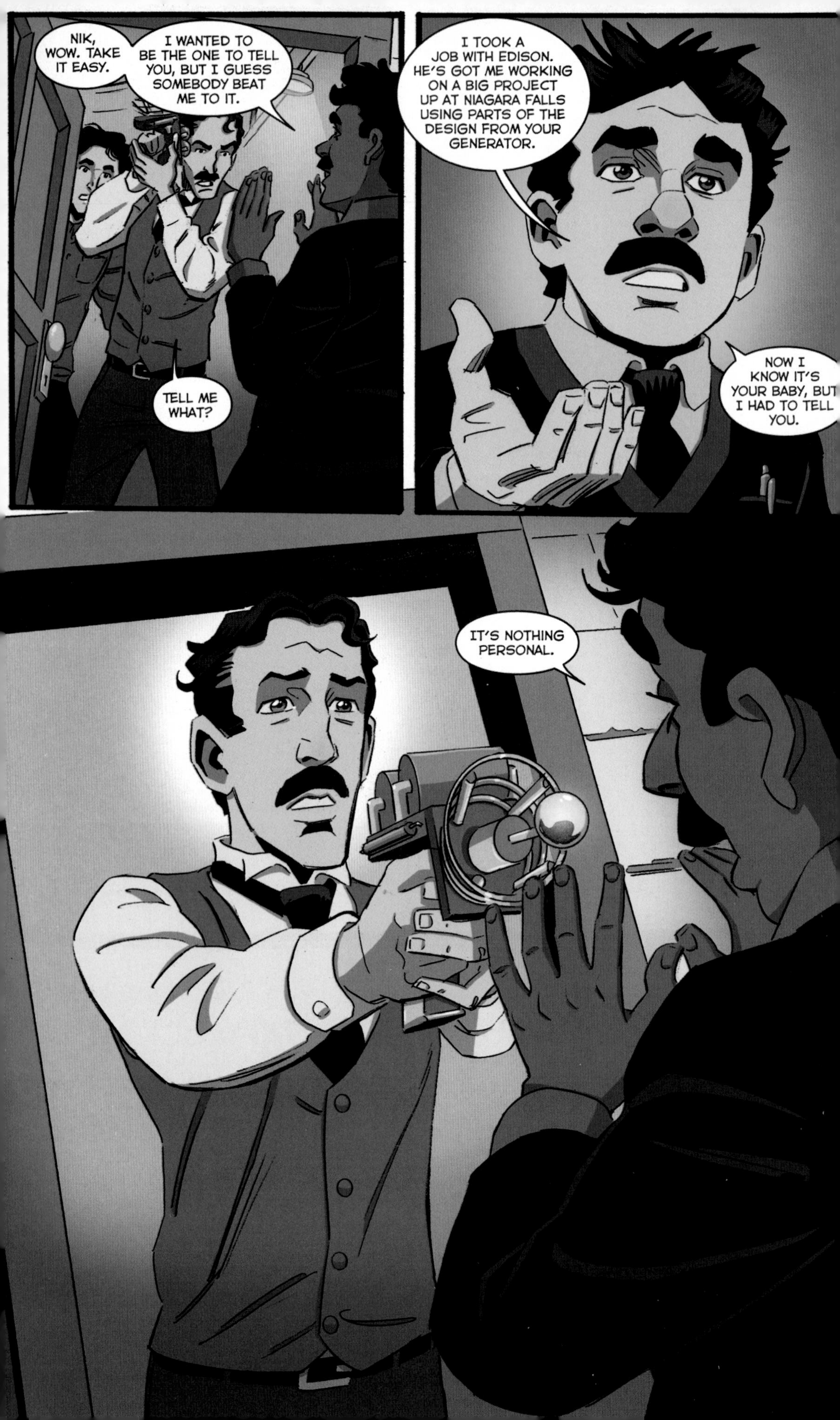
NIK, WOW. TAKE IT EASY.
I WANTED TO BE THE ONE TO TELL YOU, BUT I GUESS SOMEBODY BEAT ME TO IT.
TELL ME WHAT?
I TOOK A JOB WITH EDISON. HE'S GOT ME WORKING ON A BIG PROJECT UP AT NIAGARA FALLS USING PARTS OF THE DESIGN FROM YOUR GENERATOR.
NOW I KNOW IT'S YOUR BABY, BUT I HAD TO TELL YOU.
IT'S NOTHING PERSONAL.

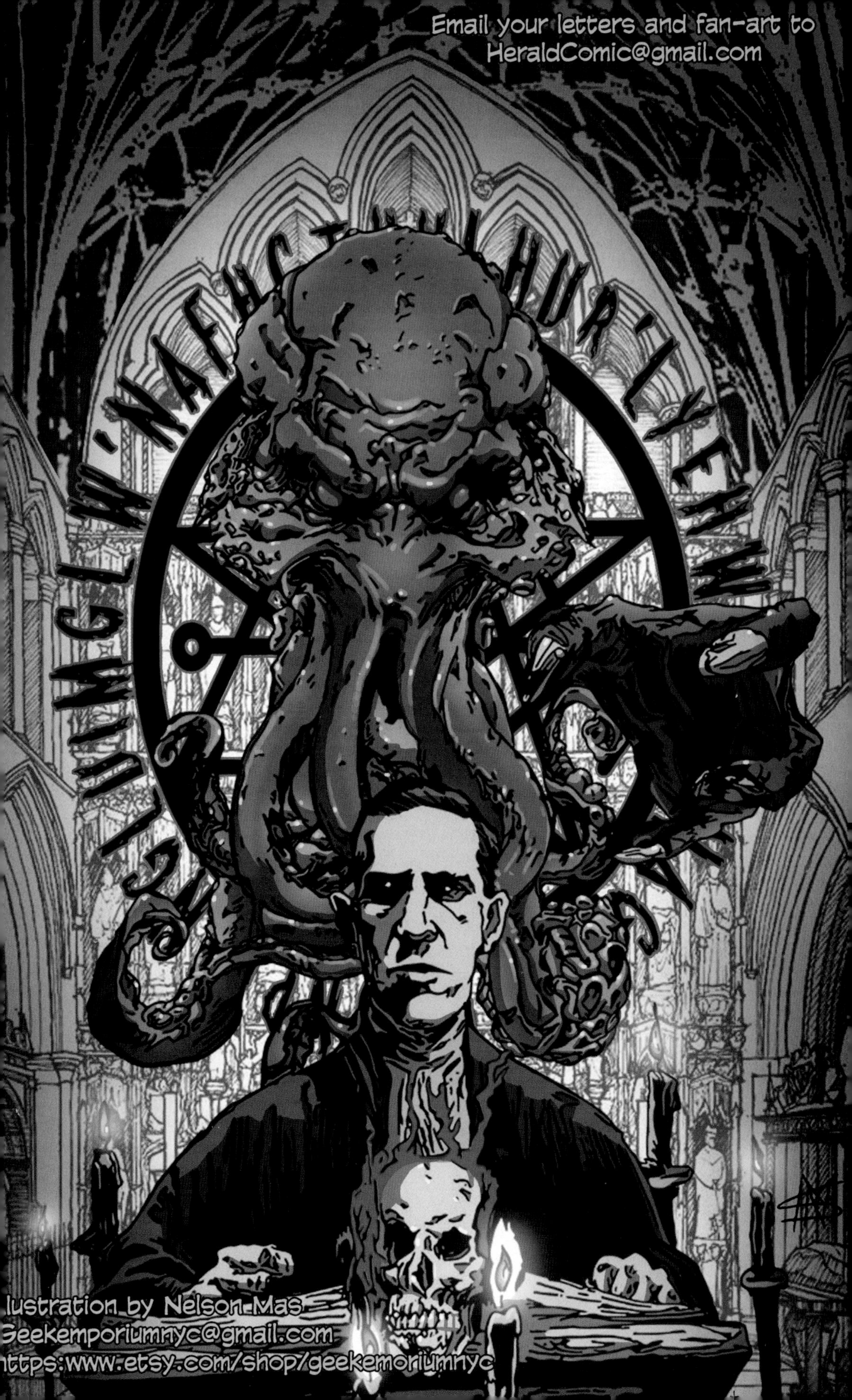

Email your letters and fan-art to
HeraldComic@gmail.com
llustration by Nelson Mas
Geekemporiumnyc@gmail.com
nttps:www.etsy.com/shop/geekemoriumnyc

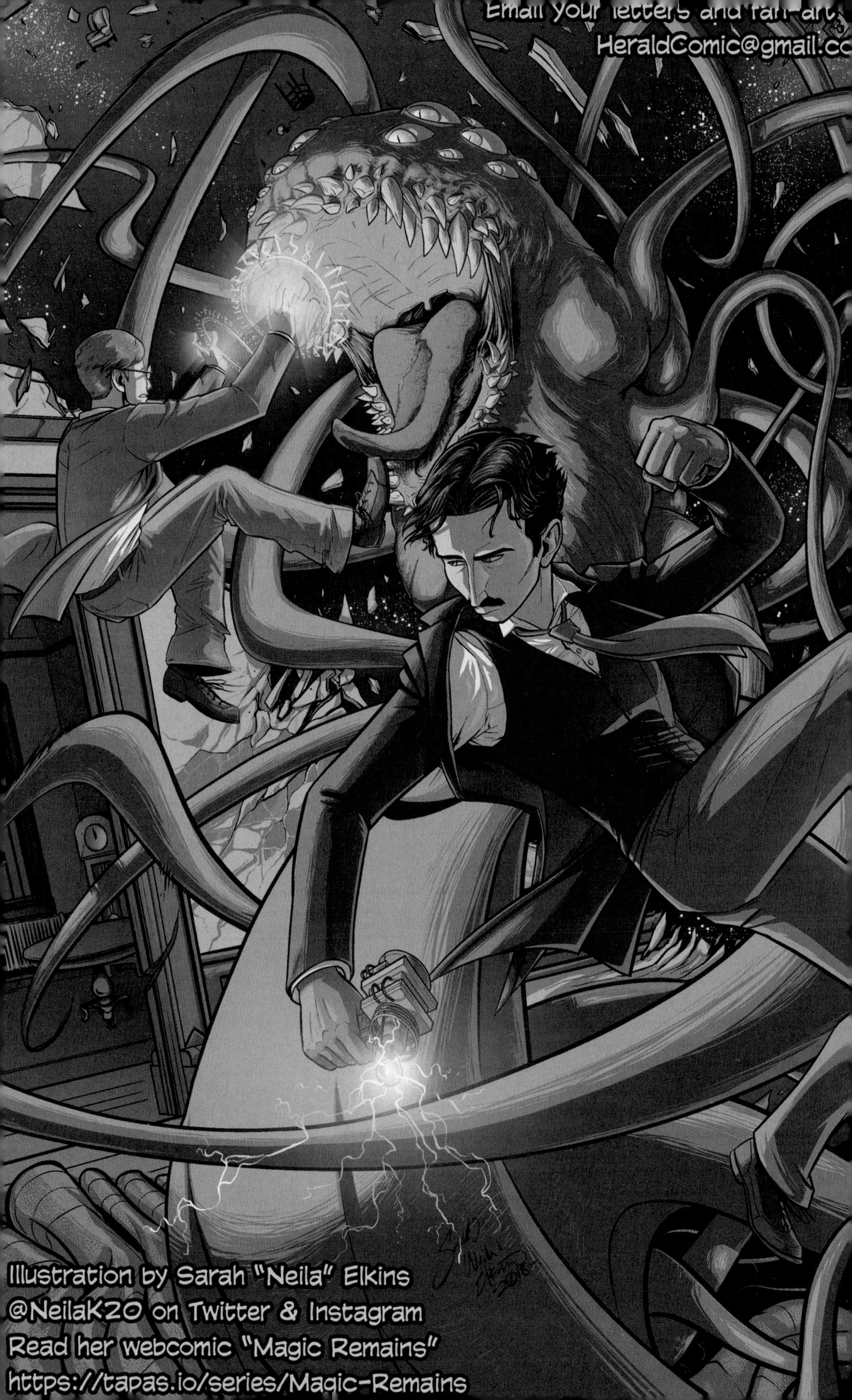
Email your letters and fan-art
HeraldComic@gmail.co
Illustration by Sarah "Neila" Elkins
@NeilaK20 on Twitter & Instagram
Read her webcomic "Magic Remains"
https://tapas.io/series/Magic-Remains

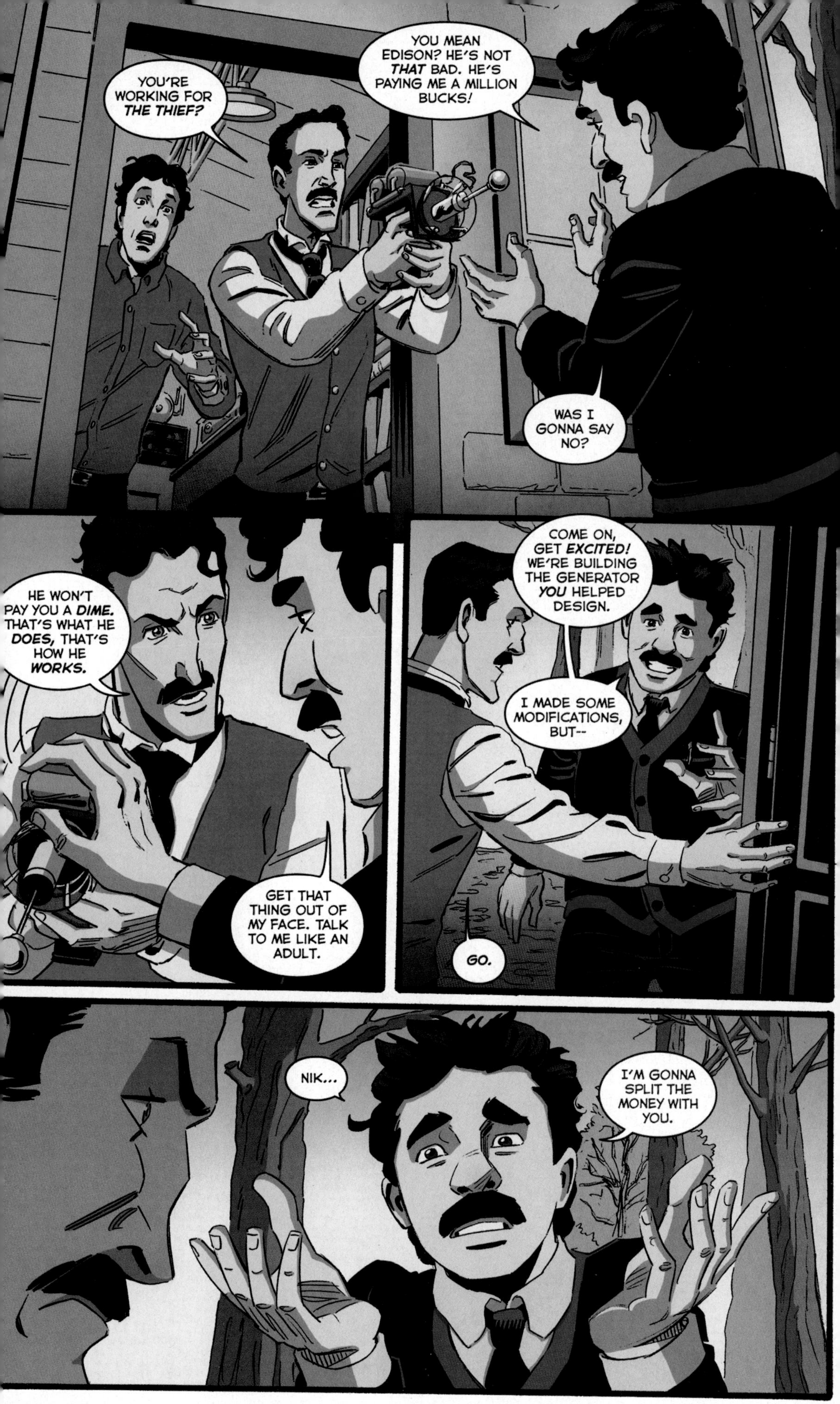
YOU'RE WORKING FOR THE THIEF?
YOU MEAN EDISON? HE'S NOT THAT BAD. HE'S PAYING ME A MILLION BUCKS!
WAS I GONNA SAY NO?
HE WON'T PAY YOU A DIME. THAT'S WHAT HE DOES, THAT'S HOW HE WORKS.
GET THAT THING OUT OF MY FACE. TALK TO ME LIKE AN ADULT.
COME ON, GET EXCITED! WE'RE BUILDING THE GENERATOR YOU HELPED DESIGN.
I MADE SOME MODIFICATIONS, BUT--
GO.
NIK...
I'M GONNA SPLIT THE MONEY WITH YOU.

IF I SEE YOU AGAIN, I MIGHT KILL YOU.

NIK, COME ON. I CAN'T KEEP WORKING IN THAT PATENT OFFICE THE REST OF MY LIFE.

YOU CAN UNDERSTAND THAT BETTER THAN ANYONE.

SLAM!

YOU'VE GOT A LITTLE TEMPER ON YOU, DON'T YOU?

IT'S MY DESIGN, I CREATED IT. HE HAS NO RIGHT GIVING IT TO THE THIEF.

WHO?

I REFUSE TO SAY HIS NAME, BUT HE THREW ME OUT OF MY WORKSHOP WHEN AMELIA NEEDED ME THE MOST. AND ONCE SHE'S HOME, I'M HOLDING HIM PERSONALLY ACCOUNTABLE.

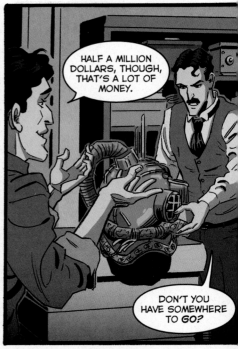

HALF A MILLION DOLLARS, THOUGH, THAT'S A LOT OF MONEY.

DON'T YOU HAVE SOMEWHERE TO GO?

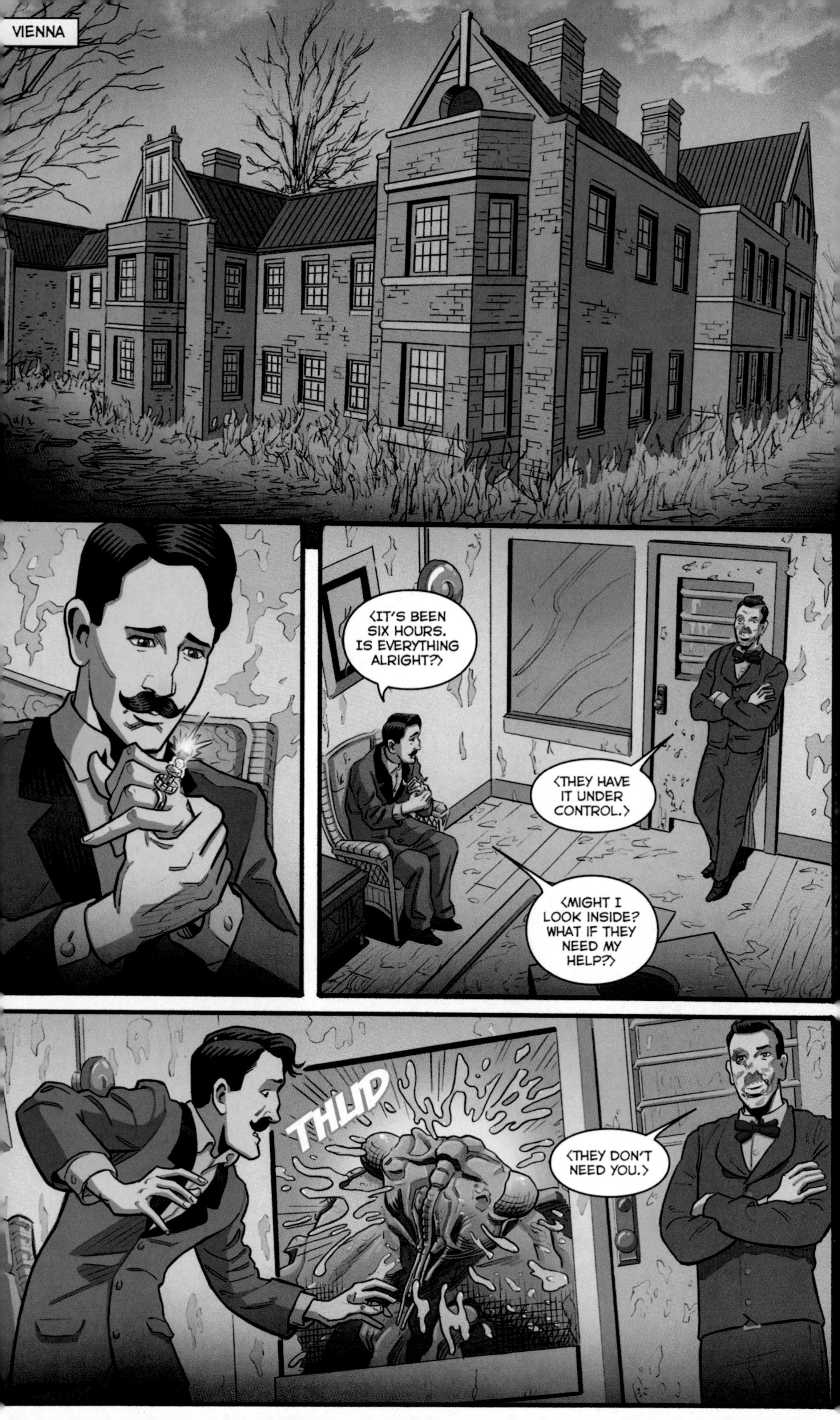
VIENNA
<IT'S BEEN SIX HOURS. IS EVERYTHING ALRIGHT?>
<THEY HAVE IT UNDER CONTROL.>
<MIGHT I LOOK INSIDE? WHAT IF THEY NEED MY HELP?>
THUD
<THEY DON'T NEED YOU.>

⟨NOT FOR THIS, AT LEAST.⟩

⟨DO YOU KNOW WHO I AM?⟩

⟨YES, SIR, I DO, AND UNLESS YOU WANT--⟩

⟨--THIS?⟩

⟨THEN YOU CAN WAIT.⟩

⟨DON'T WORRY.⟩

⟨DID IT WORK?⟩

⟨CONGRATULATIONS, WE FOUND HIM.⟩

⟨THIS...IS HIM?⟩

⟨NO, CHILD, BUT IT'S ATTUNED TO HIM.⟩

⟨THEN WHO ARE WE TALKING ABOUT?⟩

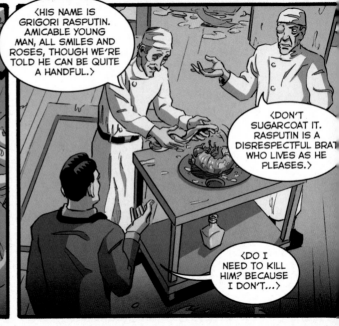

⟨HIS NAME IS GRIGORI RASPUTIN. AMICABLE YOUNG MAN, ALL SMILES AND ROSES, THOUGH WE'RE TOLD HE CAN BE QUITE A HANDFUL.⟩

⟨DON'T SUGARCOAT IT. RASPUTIN IS A DISRESPECTFUL BRAT WHO LIVES AS HE PLEASES.⟩

⟨DO I NEED TO KILL HIM? BECAUSE I DON'T...⟩

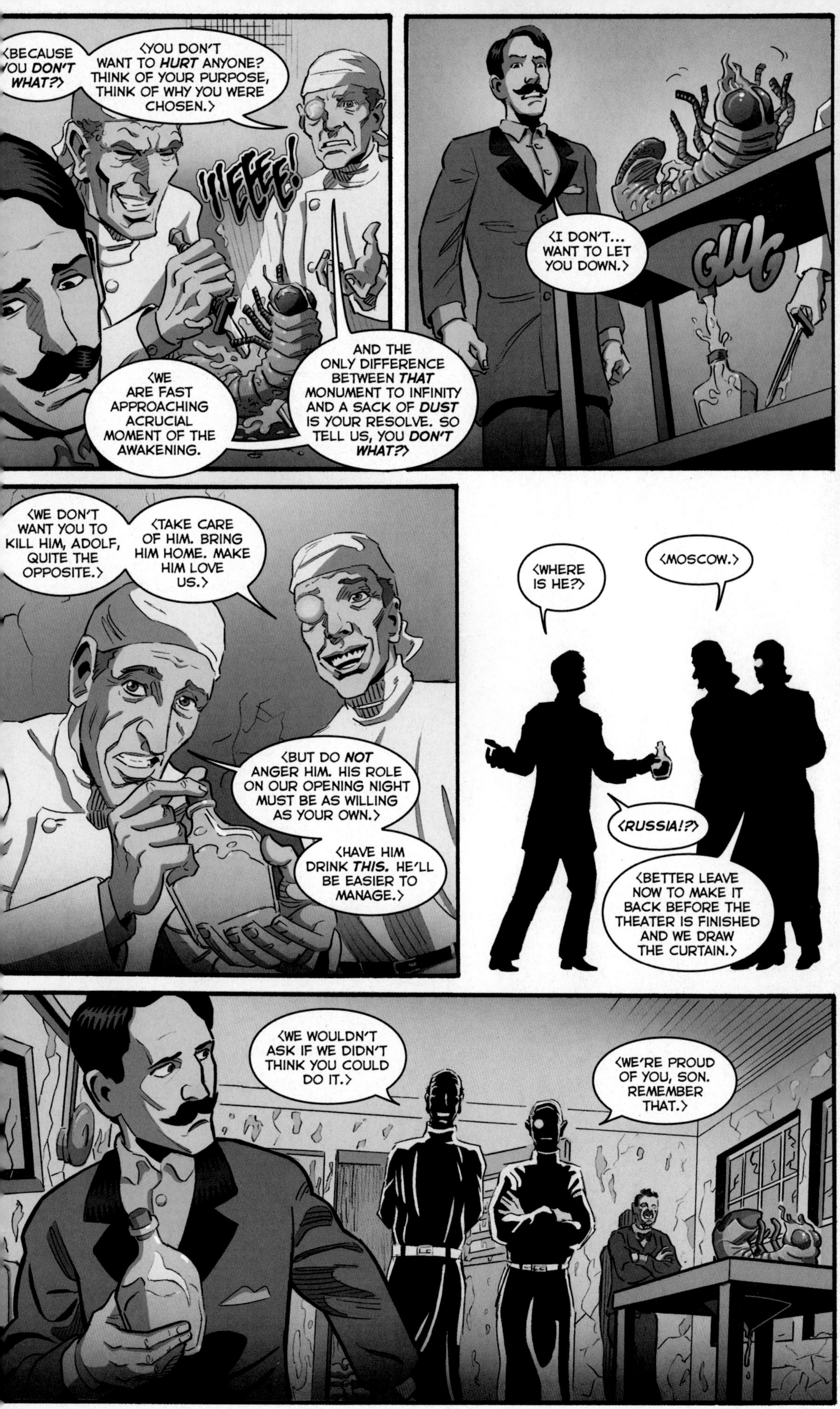

<BECAUSE YOU DON'T WHAT?>
<YOU DON'T WANT TO HURT ANYONE? THINK OF YOUR PURPOSE, THINK OF WHY YOU WERE CHOSEN.>
WEEEE!
<WE ARE FAST APPROACHING ACRUCIAL MOMENT OF THE AWAKENING.
AND THE ONLY DIFFERENCE BETWEEN THAT MONUMENT TO INFINITY AND A SACK OF DUST IS YOUR RESOLVE. SO TELL US, YOU DON'T WHAT?>
<I DON'T... WANT TO LET YOU DOWN.>
GLUG
<WE DON'T WANT YOU TO KILL HIM, ADOLF, QUITE THE OPPOSITE.>
<TAKE CARE OF HIM. BRING HIM HOME. MAKE HIM LOVE US.>
<BUT DO NOT ANGER HIM. HIS ROLE ON OUR OPENING NIGHT MUST BE AS WILLING AS YOUR OWN.>
<HAVE HIM DRINK THIS. HE'LL BE EASIER TO MANAGE.>
<WHERE IS HE?>
<MOSCOW.>
<RUSSIA!?>
<BETTER LEAVE NOW TO MAKE IT BACK BEFORE THE THEATER IS FINISHED AND WE DRAW THE CURTAIN.>
<WE WOULDN'T ASK IF WE DIDN'T THINK YOU COULD DO IT.>
<WE'RE PROUD OF YOU, SON. REMEMBER THAT.>

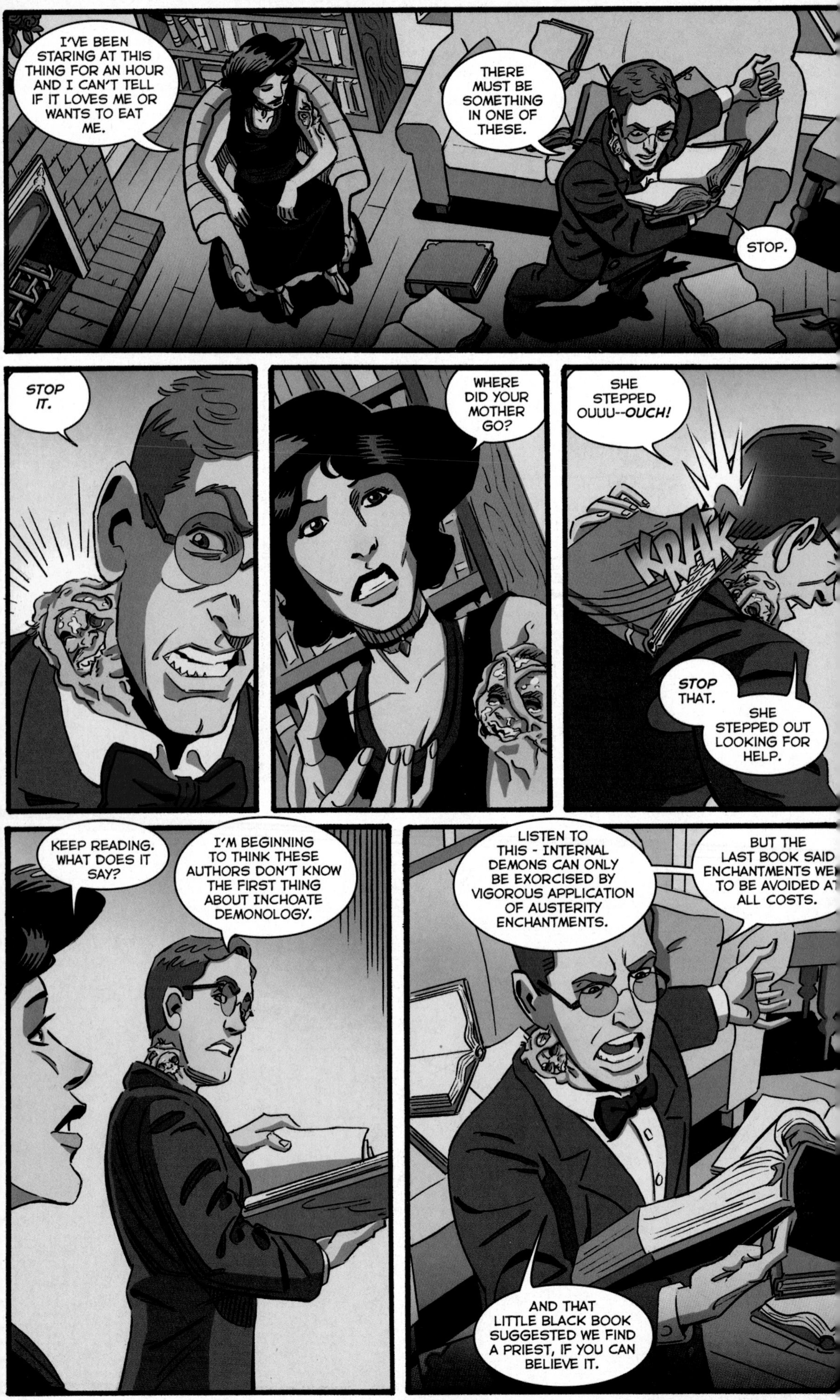
I'VE BEEN STARING AT THIS THING FOR AN HOUR AND I CAN'T TELL IF IT LOVES ME OR WANTS TO EAT ME.
THERE MUST BE SOMETHING IN ONE OF THESE.
STOP.
STOP IT.
WHERE DID YOUR MOTHER GO?
SHE STEPPED OUUU--OUCH!
KRAK
STOP THAT.
SHE STEPPED OUT LOOKING FOR HELP.
KEEP READING. WHAT DOES IT SAY?
I'M BEGINNING TO THINK THESE AUTHORS DON'T KNOW THE FIRST THING ABOUT INCHOATE DEMONOLOGY.
LISTEN TO THIS - INTERNAL DEMONS CAN ONLY BE EXORCISED BY VIGOROUS APPLICATION OF AUSTERITY ENCHANTMENTS.
BUT THE LAST BOOK SAID ENCHANTMENTS WE TO BE AVOIDED A ALL COSTS.
AND THAT LITTLE BLACK BOOK SUGGESTED WE FIND A PRIEST, IF YOU CAN BELIEVE IT.

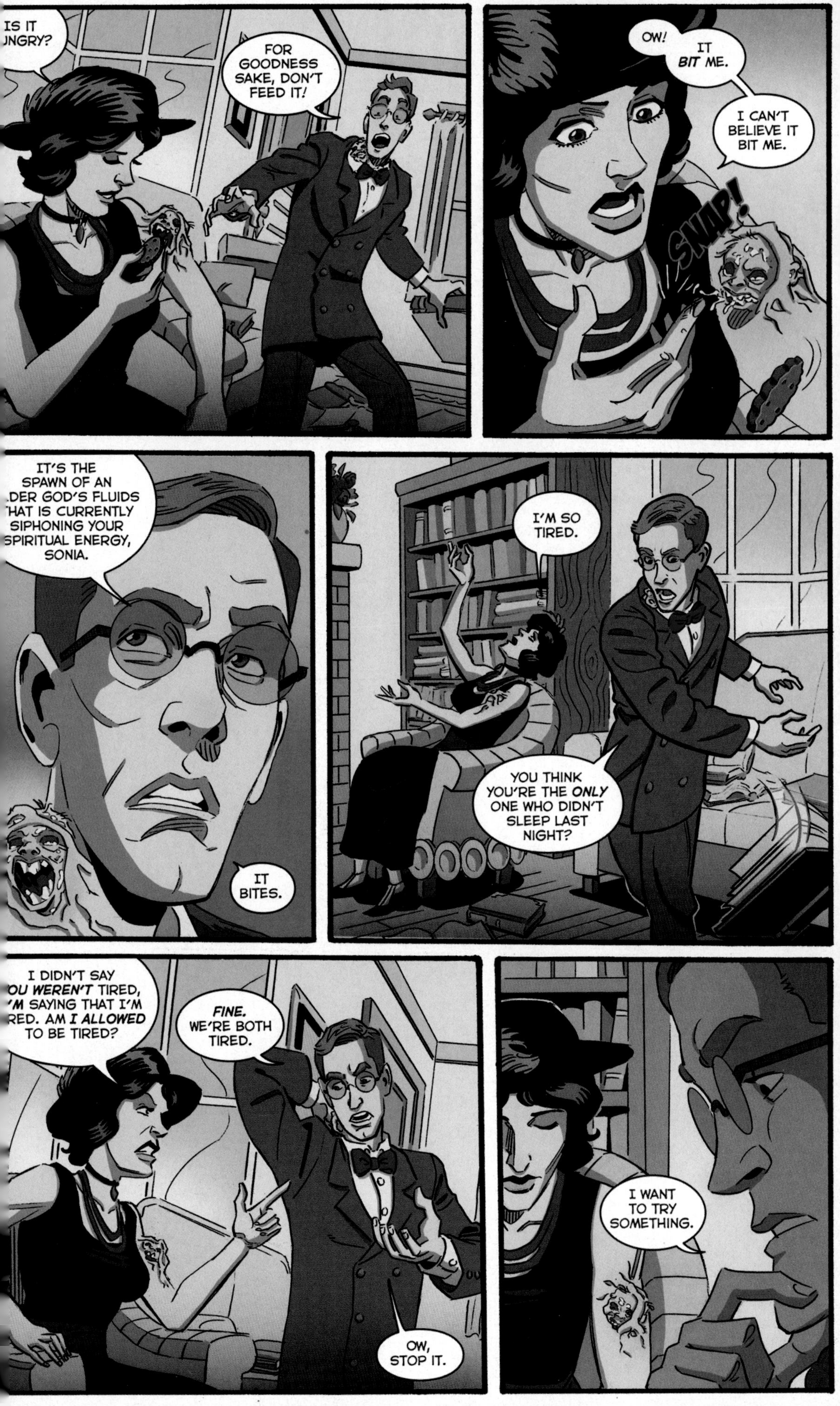

IS IT UNGRY?
FOR GOODNESS SAKE, DON'T FEED IT!
OW!
IT BIT ME.
I CAN'T BELIEVE IT BIT ME.
SNAP!
IT'S THE SPAWN OF AN LDER GOD'S FLUIDS THAT IS CURRENTLY SIPHONING YOUR SPIRITUAL ENERGY, SONIA.
IT BITES.
I'M SO TIRED.
YOU THINK YOU'RE THE ONLY ONE WHO DIDN'T SLEEP LAST NIGHT?
I DIDN'T SAY OU WEREN'T TIRED, 'M SAYING THAT I'M RED. AM I ALLOWED TO BE TIRED?
FINE. WE'RE BOTH TIRED.
OW, STOP IT.
I WANT TO TRY SOMETHING.

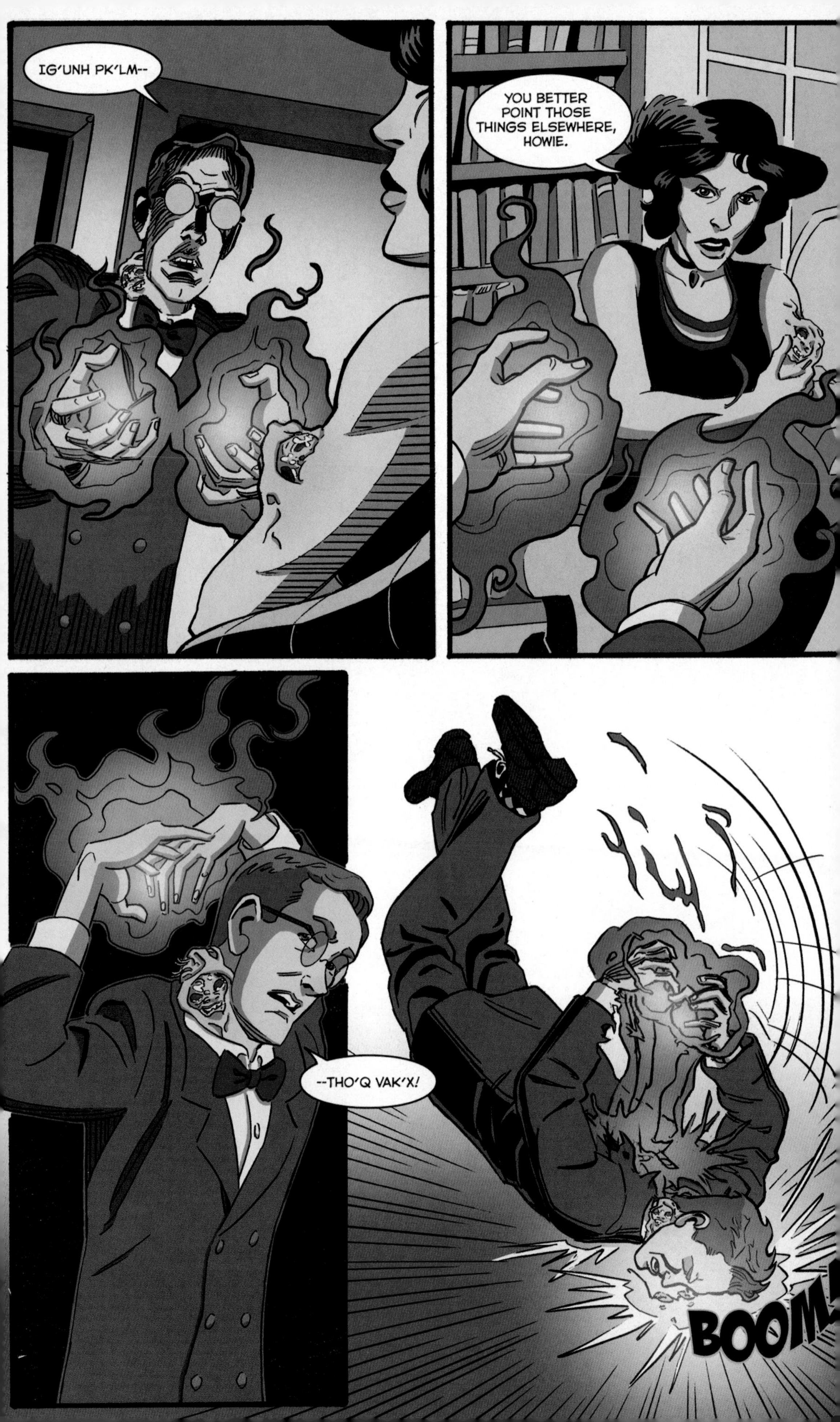
IG'UNH PK'LM--
YOU BETTER POINT THOSE THINGS ELSEWHERE, HOWIE.
--THO'Q VAK'X!
BOOM

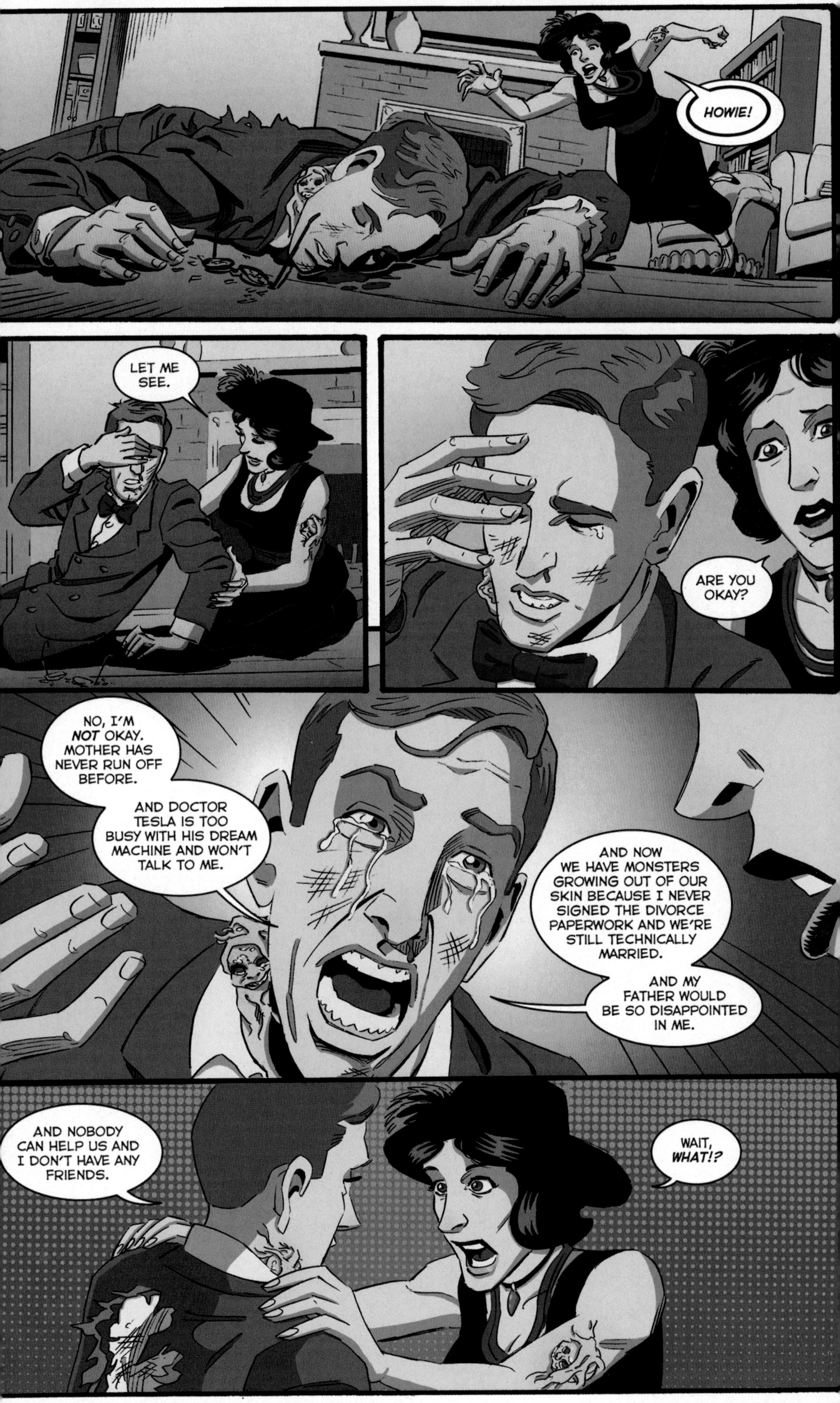
HOWIE!
LET ME SEE.
ARE YOU OKAY?
NO, I'M *NOT* OKAY. MOTHER HAS NEVER RUN OFF BEFORE.
AND DOCTOR TESLA IS TOO BUSY WITH HIS DREAM MACHINE AND WON'T TALK TO ME.
AND NOW WE HAVE MONSTERS GROWING OUT OF OUR SKIN BECAUSE I NEVER SIGNED THE DIVORCE PAPERWORK AND WE'RE STILL TECHNICALLY MARRIED.
AND MY FATHER WOULD BE SO DISAPPOINTED IN ME.
AND NOBODY CAN HELP US AND I DON'T HAVE ANY FRIENDS.
WAIT, *WHAT!?*

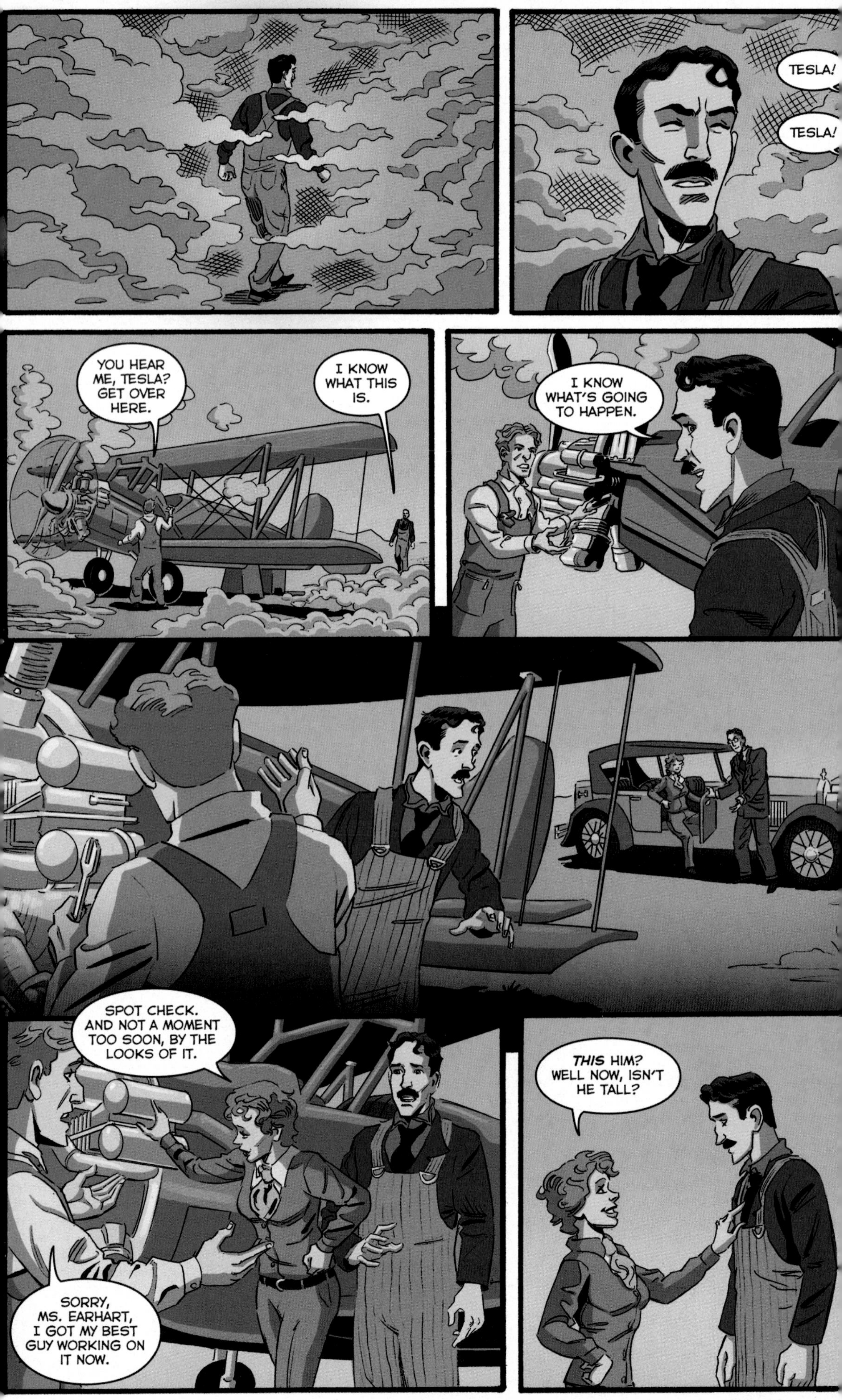
TESLA!
TESLA!
YOU HEAR ME, TESLA? GET OVER HERE.
I KNOW WHAT THIS IS.
I KNOW WHAT'S GOING TO HAPPEN.
SPOT CHECK. AND NOT A MOMENT TOO SOON, BY THE LOOKS OF IT.
SORRY, MS. EARHART, I GOT MY BEST GUY WORKING ON IT NOW.
THIS HIM? WELL NOW, ISN'T HE TALL?

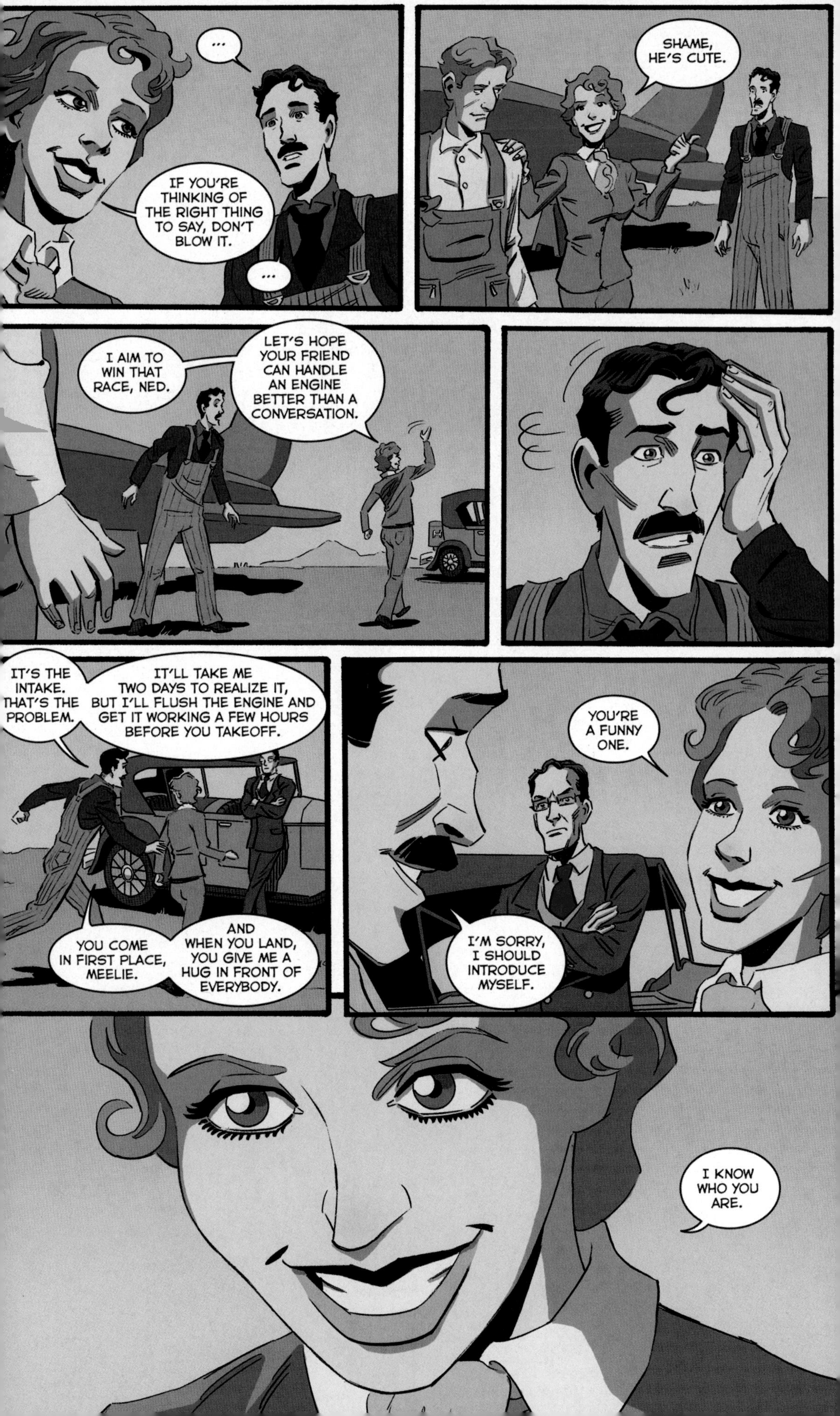
...
IF YOU'RE THINKING OF THE RIGHT THING TO SAY, DON'T BLOW IT.
...
SHAME, HE'S CUTE.
I AIM TO WIN THAT RACE, NED.
LET'S HOPE YOUR FRIEND CAN HANDLE AN ENGINE BETTER THAN A CONVERSATION.
IT'S THE INTAKE. THAT'S THE PROBLEM.
IT'LL TAKE ME TWO DAYS TO REALIZE IT, BUT I'LL FLUSH THE ENGINE AND GET IT WORKING A FEW HOURS BEFORE YOU TAKEOFF.
YOU COME IN FIRST PLACE, MEELIE.
AND WHEN YOU LAND, YOU GIVE ME A HUG IN FRONT OF EVERYBODY.
YOU'RE A FUNNY ONE.
I'M SORRY, I SHOULD INTRODUCE MYSELF.
I KNOW WHO YOU ARE.

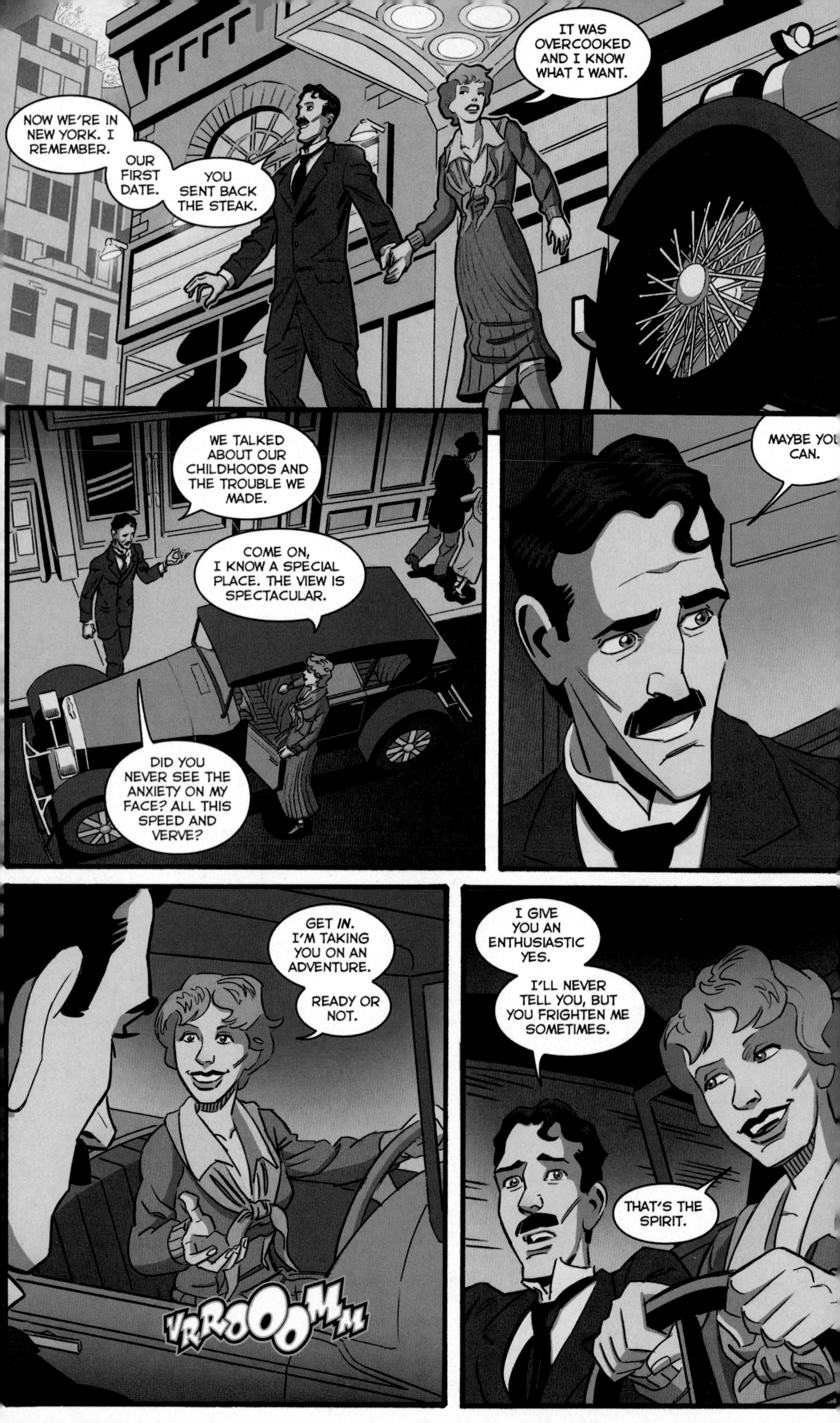
NOW WE'RE IN NEW YORK. I REMEMBER.
OUR FIRST DATE.
YOU SENT BACK THE STEAK.
IT WAS OVERCOOKED AND I KNOW WHAT I WANT.
WE TALKED ABOUT OUR CHILDHOODS AND THE TROUBLE WE MADE.
COME ON, I KNOW A SPECIAL PLACE. THE VIEW IS SPECTACULAR.
DID YOU NEVER SEE THE ANXIETY ON MY FACE? ALL THIS SPEED AND VERVE?
MAYBE YOU CAN.
GET *IN*. I'M TAKING YOU ON AN ADVENTURE.
READY OR NOT.
VRRROOOOMMM
I GIVE YOU AN ENTHUSIASTIC YES.
I'LL NEVER TELL YOU, BUT YOU FRIGHTEN ME SOMETIMES.
THAT'S THE SPIRIT.

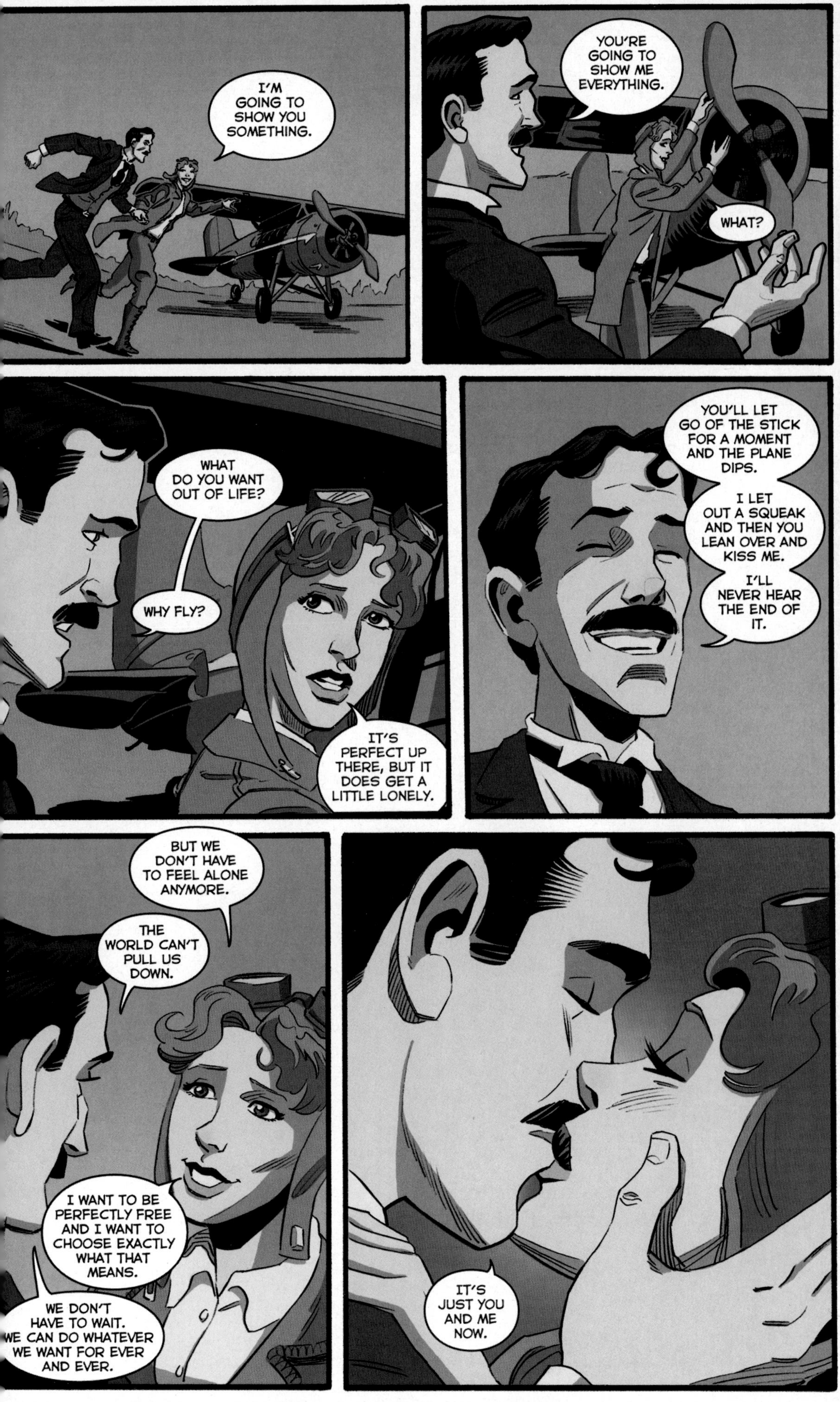
I'M GOING TO SHOW YOU SOMETHING.
YOU'RE GOING TO SHOW ME EVERYTHING.
WHAT?
WHAT DO YOU WANT OUT OF LIFE?
WHY FLY?
IT'S PERFECT UP THERE, BUT IT DOES GET A LITTLE LONELY.
YOU'LL LET GO OF THE STICK FOR A MOMENT AND THE PLANE DIPS.
I LET OUT A SQUEAK AND THEN YOU LEAN OVER AND KISS ME.
I'LL NEVER HEAR THE END OF IT.
BUT WE DON'T HAVE TO FEEL ALONE ANYMORE.
THE WORLD CAN'T PULL US DOWN.
I WANT TO BE PERFECTLY FREE AND I WANT TO CHOOSE EXACTLY WHAT THAT MEANS.
WE DON'T HAVE TO WAIT. WE CAN DO WHATEVER WE WANT FOR EVER AND EVER.
IT'S JUST YOU AND ME NOW.

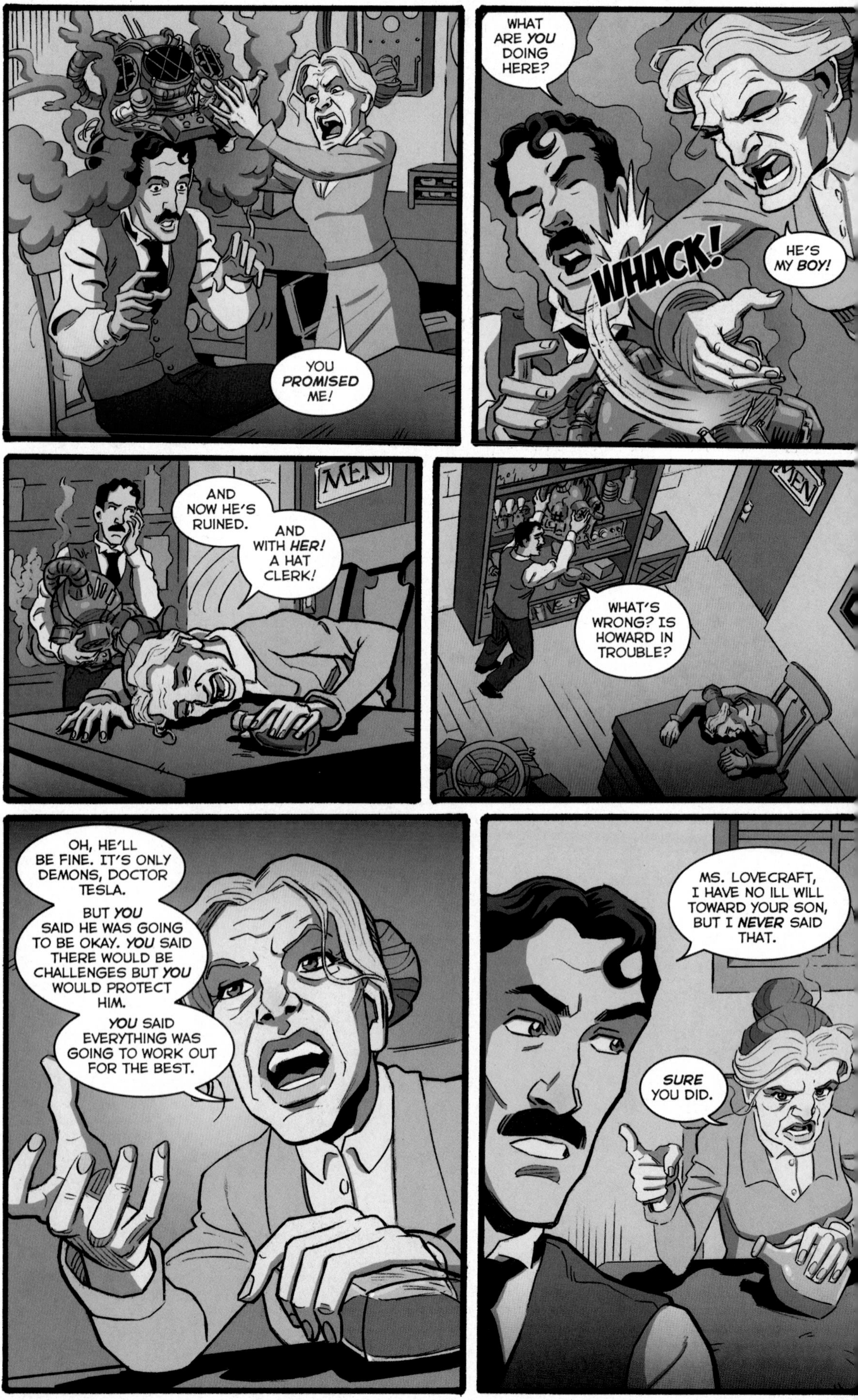

YOU *PROMISED* ME!
WHAT ARE *YOU* DOING HERE?
WHACK!
HE'S MY *BOY!*
AND NOW HE'S RUINED.
AND WITH *HER!* A HAT CLERK!
WHAT'S WRONG? IS HOWARD IN TROUBLE?
OH, HE'LL BE FINE. IT'S ONLY DEMONS, DOCTOR TESLA.
BUT *YOU* SAID HE WAS GOING TO BE OKAY. *YOU* SAID THERE WOULD BE CHALLENGES BUT *YOU* WOULD PROTECT HIM.
YOU SAID EVERYTHING WAS GOING TO WORK OUT FOR THE BEST.
MS. LOVECRAFT, I HAVE NO ILL WILL TOWARD YOUR SON, BUT I *NEVER* SAID THAT.
SURE YOU DID.

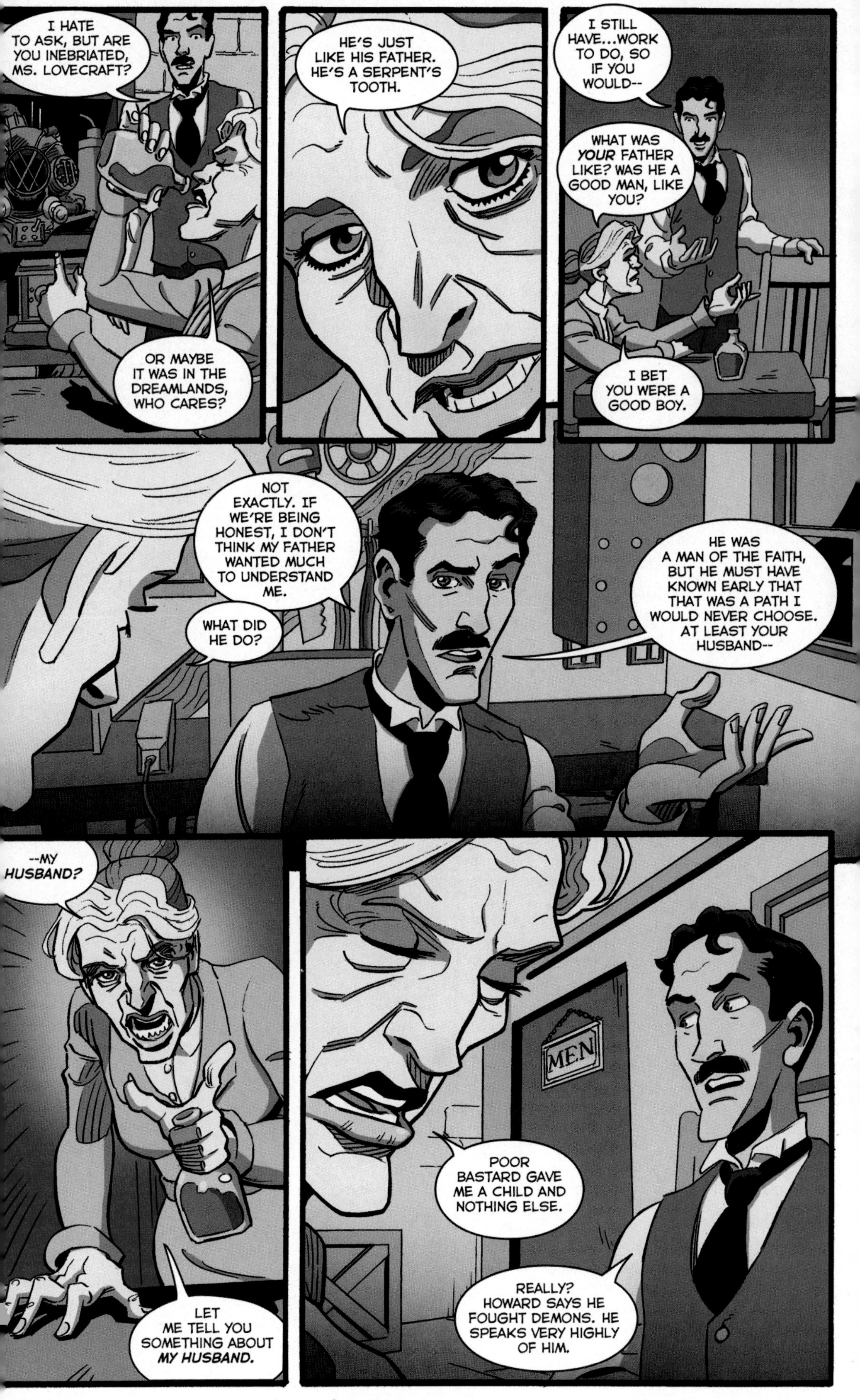
I HATE TO ASK, BUT ARE YOU INEBRIATED, MS. LOVECRAFT?
OR MAYBE IT WAS IN THE DREAMLANDS, WHO CARES?
HE'S JUST LIKE HIS FATHER. HE'S A SERPENT'S TOOTH.
I STILL HAVE...WORK TO DO, SO IF YOU WOULD--
WHAT WAS YOUR FATHER LIKE? WAS HE A GOOD MAN, LIKE YOU?
I BET YOU WERE A GOOD BOY.
NOT EXACTLY. IF WE'RE BEING HONEST, I DON'T THINK MY FATHER WANTED MUCH TO UNDERSTAND ME.
WHAT DID HE DO?
HE WAS A MAN OF THE FAITH, BUT HE MUST HAVE KNOWN EARLY THAT THAT WAS A PATH I WOULD NEVER CHOOSE. AT LEAST YOUR HUSBAND--
--MY HUSBAND?
LET ME TELL YOU SOMETHING ABOUT MY HUSBAND.
MEN
POOR BASTARD GAVE ME A CHILD AND NOTHING ELSE.
REALLY? HOWARD SAYS HE FOUGHT DEMONS. HE SPEAKS VERY HIGHLY OF HIM.

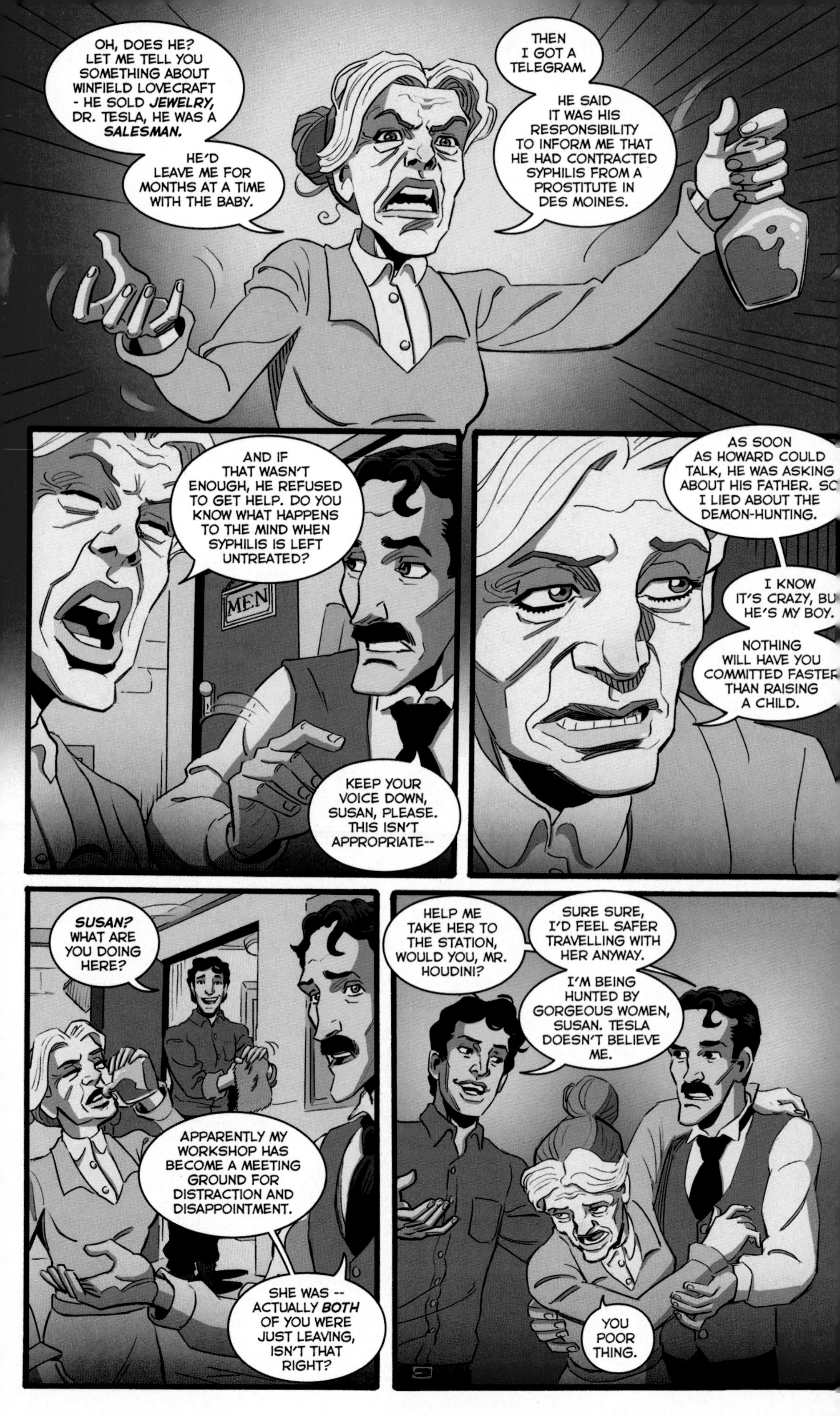
OH, DOES HE? LET ME TELL YOU SOMETHING ABOUT WINFIELD LOVECRAFT - HE SOLD *JEWELRY,* DR. TESLA, HE WAS A *SALESMAN.*
HE'D LEAVE ME FOR MONTHS AT A TIME WITH THE BABY.
THEN I GOT A TELEGRAM.
HE SAID IT WAS HIS RESPONSIBILITY TO INFORM ME THAT HE HAD CONTRACTED SYPHILIS FROM A PROSTITUTE IN DES MOINES.
AND IF THAT WASN'T ENOUGH, HE REFUSED TO GET HELP. DO YOU KNOW WHAT HAPPENS TO THE MIND WHEN SYPHILIS IS LEFT UNTREATED?
MEN
KEEP YOUR VOICE DOWN, SUSAN, PLEASE. THIS ISN'T APPROPRIATE--
AS SOON AS HOWARD COULD TALK, HE WAS ASKING ABOUT HIS FATHER. SO I LIED ABOUT THE DEMON-HUNTING.
I KNOW IT'S CRAZY, BU HE'S MY BOY.
NOTHING WILL HAVE YOU COMMITTED FASTER THAN RAISING A CHILD.
SUSAN? WHAT ARE YOU DOING HERE?
APPARENTLY MY WORKSHOP HAS BECOME A MEETING GROUND FOR DISTRACTION AND DISAPPOINTMENT.
SHE WAS -- ACTUALLY *BOTH* OF YOU WERE JUST LEAVING, ISN'T THAT RIGHT?
HELP ME TAKE HER TO THE STATION, WOULD YOU, MR. HOUDINI?
SURE SURE, I'D FEEL SAFER TRAVELLING WITH HER ANYWAY.
I'M BEING HUNTED BY GORGEOUS WOMEN, SUSAN. TESLA DOESN'T BELIEVE ME.
YOU POOR THING.

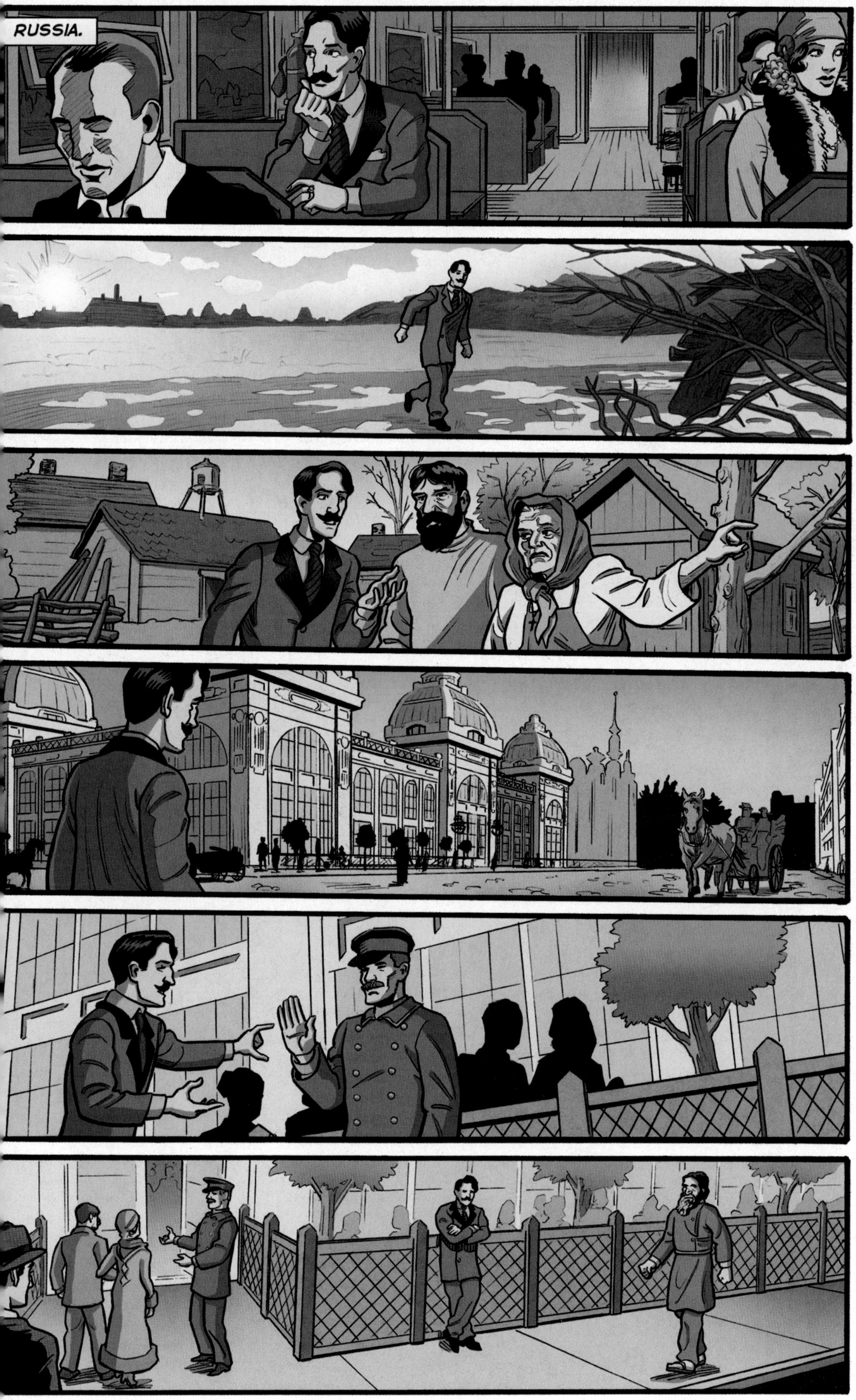
RUSSIA.

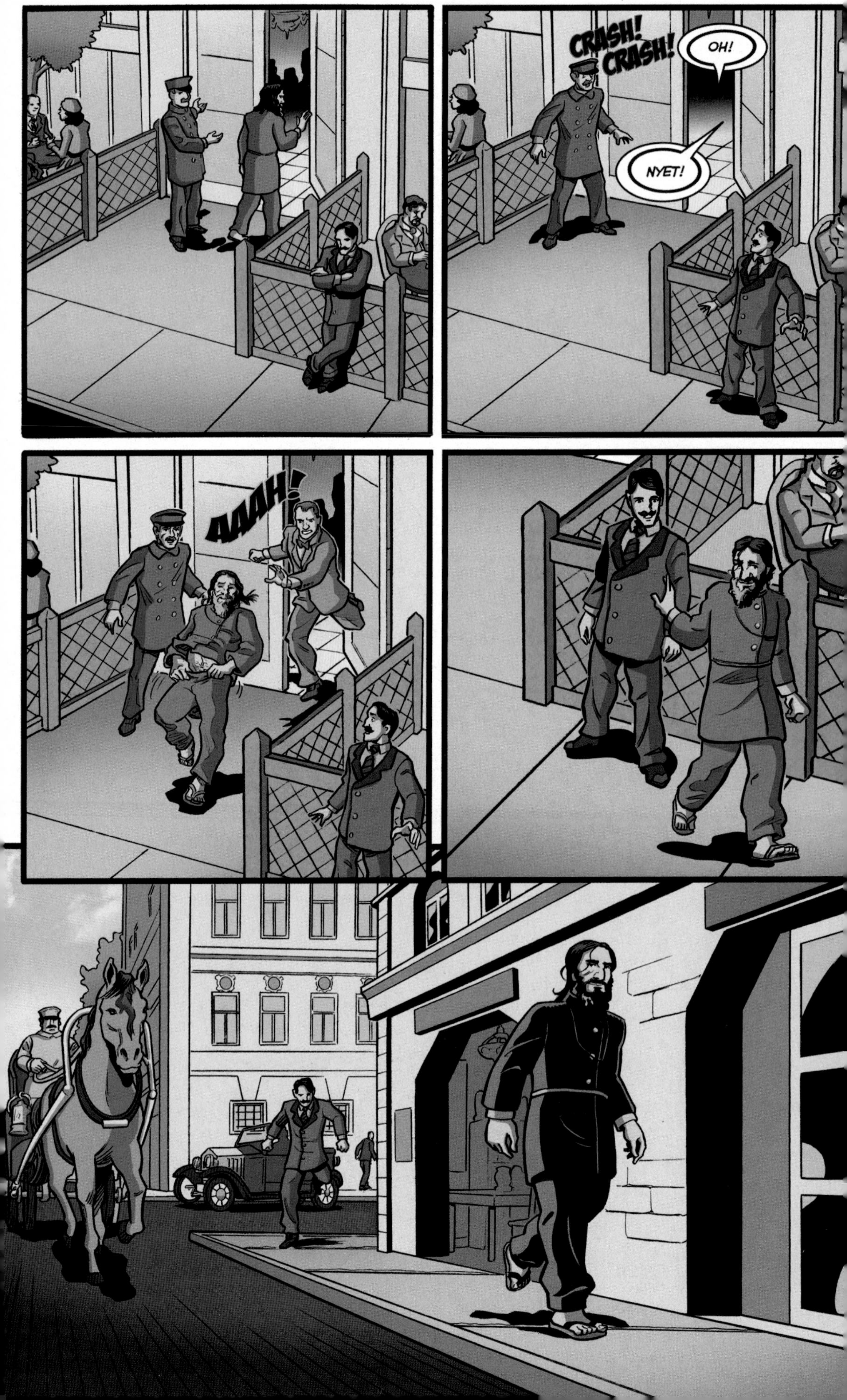
CRASH!
CRASH!
OH!
NYET!
AAAH!

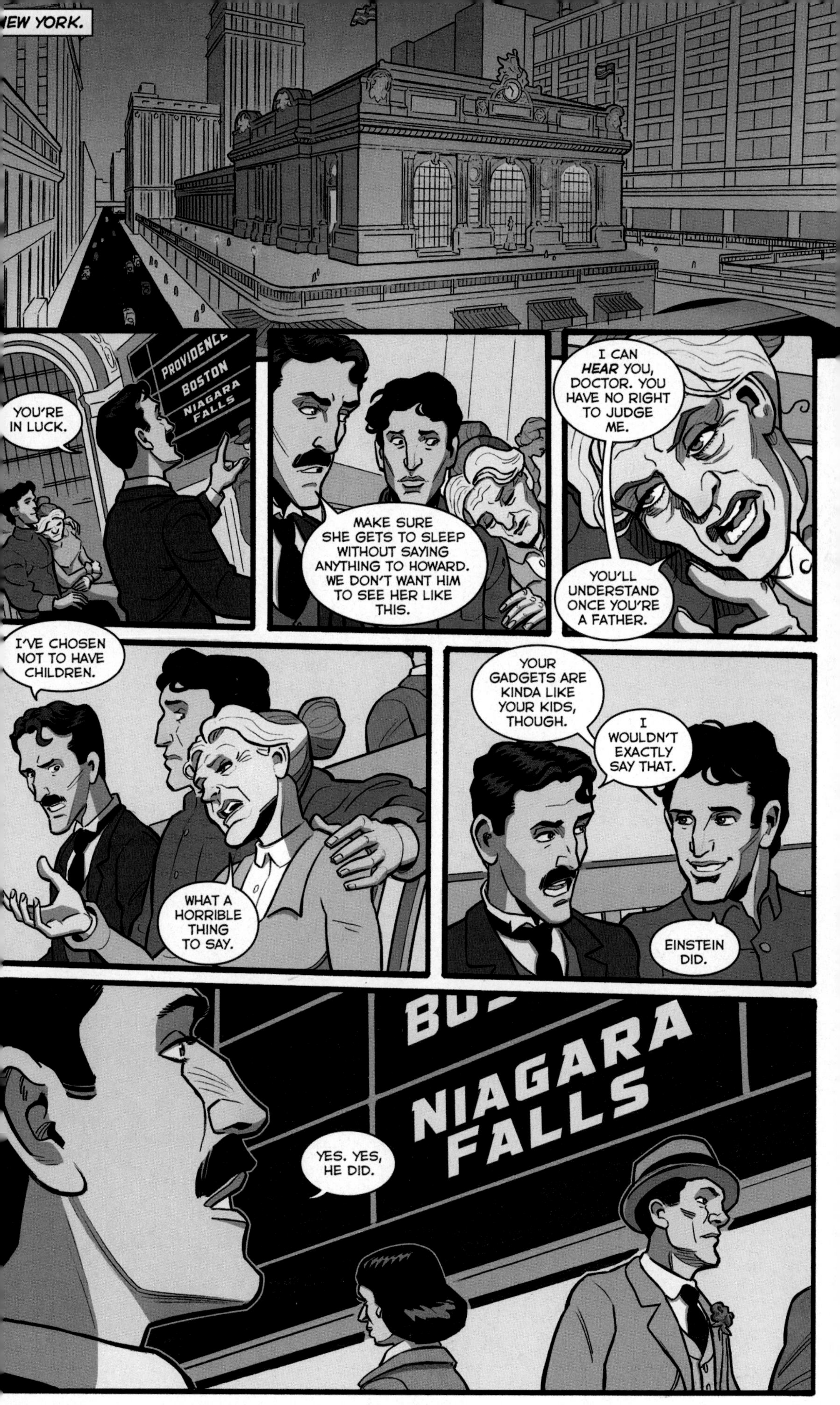
NEW YORK.
PROVIDENCE
BOSTON
NIAGARA FALLS
YOU'RE IN LUCK.
MAKE SURE SHE GETS TO SLEEP WITHOUT SAYING ANYTHING TO HOWARD. WE DON'T WANT HIM TO SEE HER LIKE THIS.
I CAN *HEAR* YOU, DOCTOR. YOU HAVE NO RIGHT TO JUDGE ME.
YOU'LL UNDERSTAND ONCE YOU'RE A FATHER.
I'VE CHOSEN NOT TO HAVE CHILDREN.
WHAT A HORRIBLE THING TO SAY.
YOUR GADGETS ARE KINDA LIKE YOUR KIDS, THOUGH.
I WOULDN'T EXACTLY SAY THAT.
EINSTEIN DID.
NIAGARA FALLS
YES. YES, HE DID.

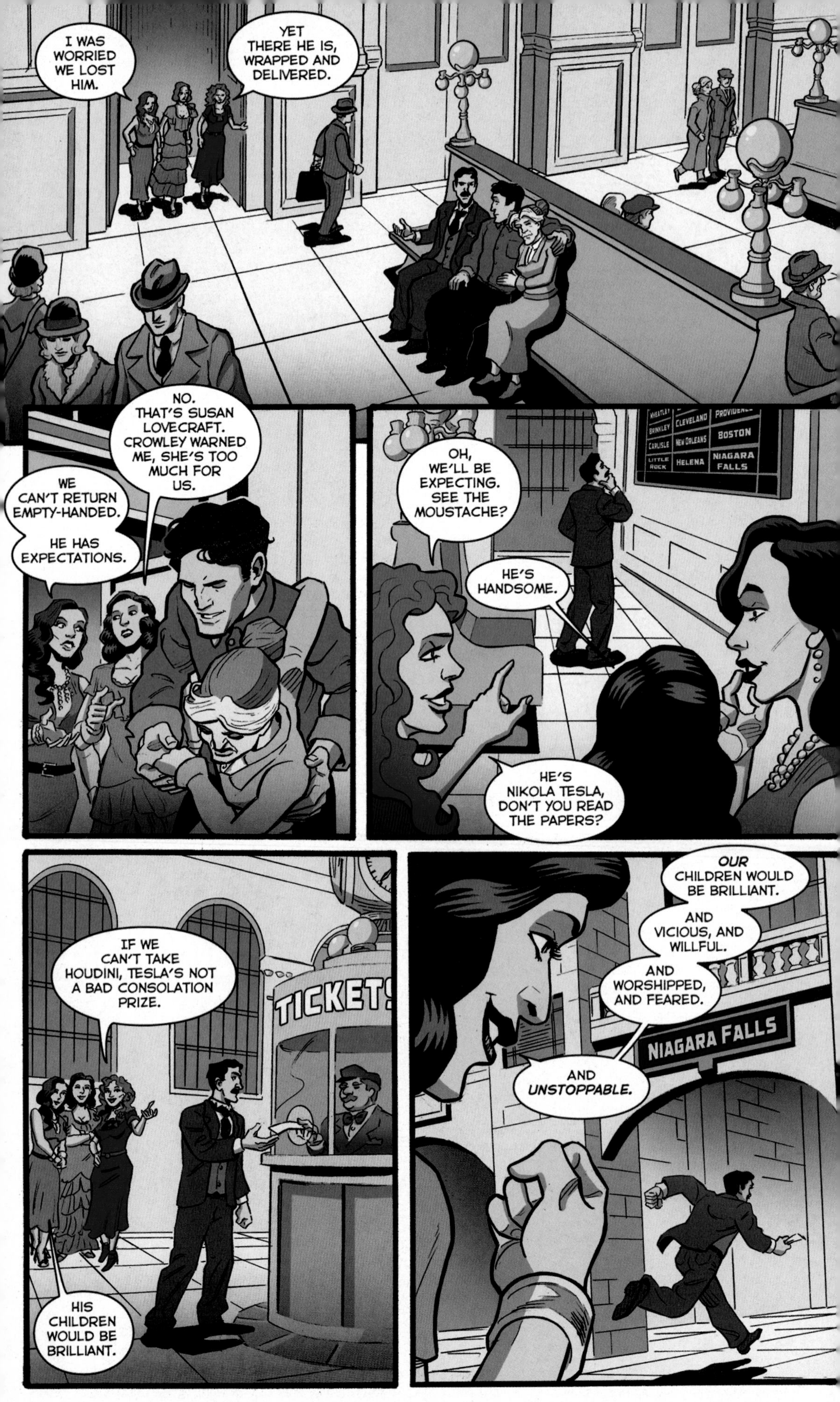
I WAS WORRIED WE LOST HIM.
YET THERE HE IS, WRAPPED AND DELIVERED.
WE CAN'T RETURN EMPTY-HANDED.
HE HAS EXPECTATIONS.
NO. THAT'S SUSAN LOVECRAFT. CROWLEY WARNED ME, SHE'S TOO MUCH FOR US.
WHEATLEY
BRINKLEY
CLEVELAND
PROVIDENCE
CARLISLE
NEW ORLEANS
BOSTON
LITTLE ROCK
HELENA
NIAGARA FALLS
OH, WE'LL BE EXPECTING. SEE THE MOUSTACHE?
HE'S HANDSOME.
HE'S NIKOLA TESLA, DON'T YOU READ THE PAPERS?
IF WE CAN'T TAKE HOUDINI, TESLA'S NOT A BAD CONSOLATION PRIZE.
TICKETS
HIS CHILDREN WOULD BE BRILLIANT.
OUR CHILDREN WOULD BE BRILLIANT.
AND VICIOUS, AND WILLFUL.
AND WORSHIPPED, AND FEARED.
NIAGARA FALLS
AND *UNSTOPPABLE.*

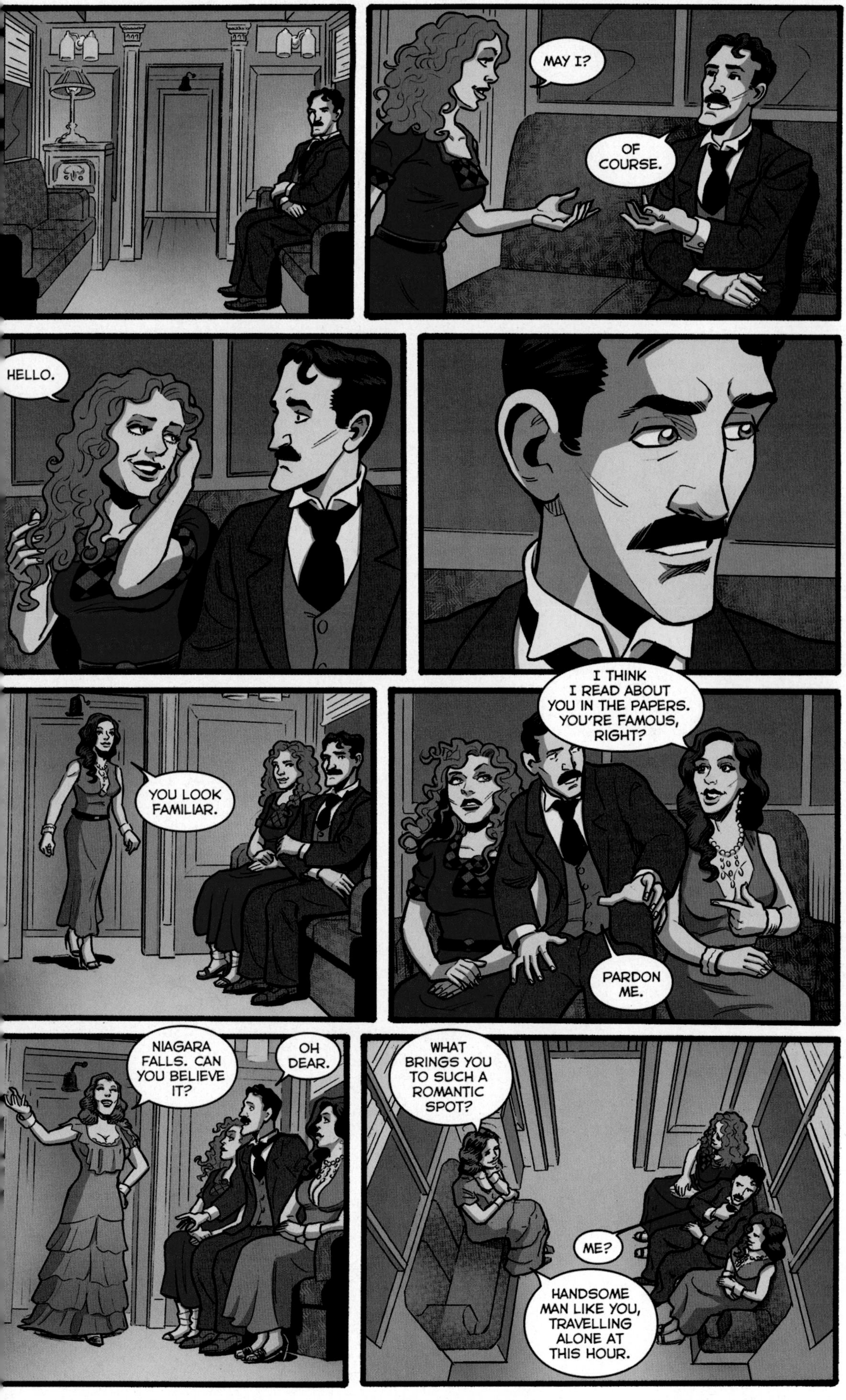
MAY I?
OF COURSE.
HELLO.
YOU LOOK FAMILIAR.
I THINK I READ ABOUT YOU IN THE PAPERS. YOU'RE FAMOUS, RIGHT?
PARDON ME.
NIAGARA FALLS. CAN YOU BELIEVE IT?
OH DEAR.
WHAT BRINGS YOU TO SUCH A ROMANTIC SPOT?
ME?
HANDSOME MAN LIKE YOU, TRAVELLING ALONE AT THIS HOUR.

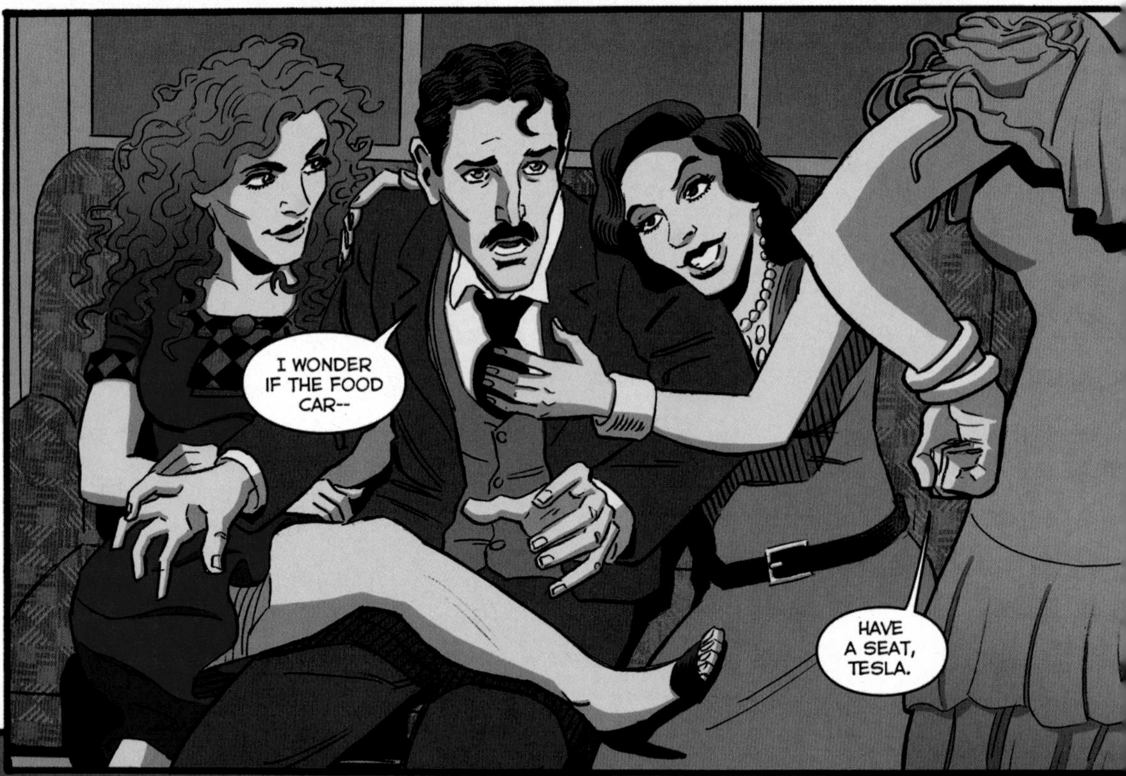
I WONDER IF THE FOOD CAR--
HAVE A SEAT, TESLA.

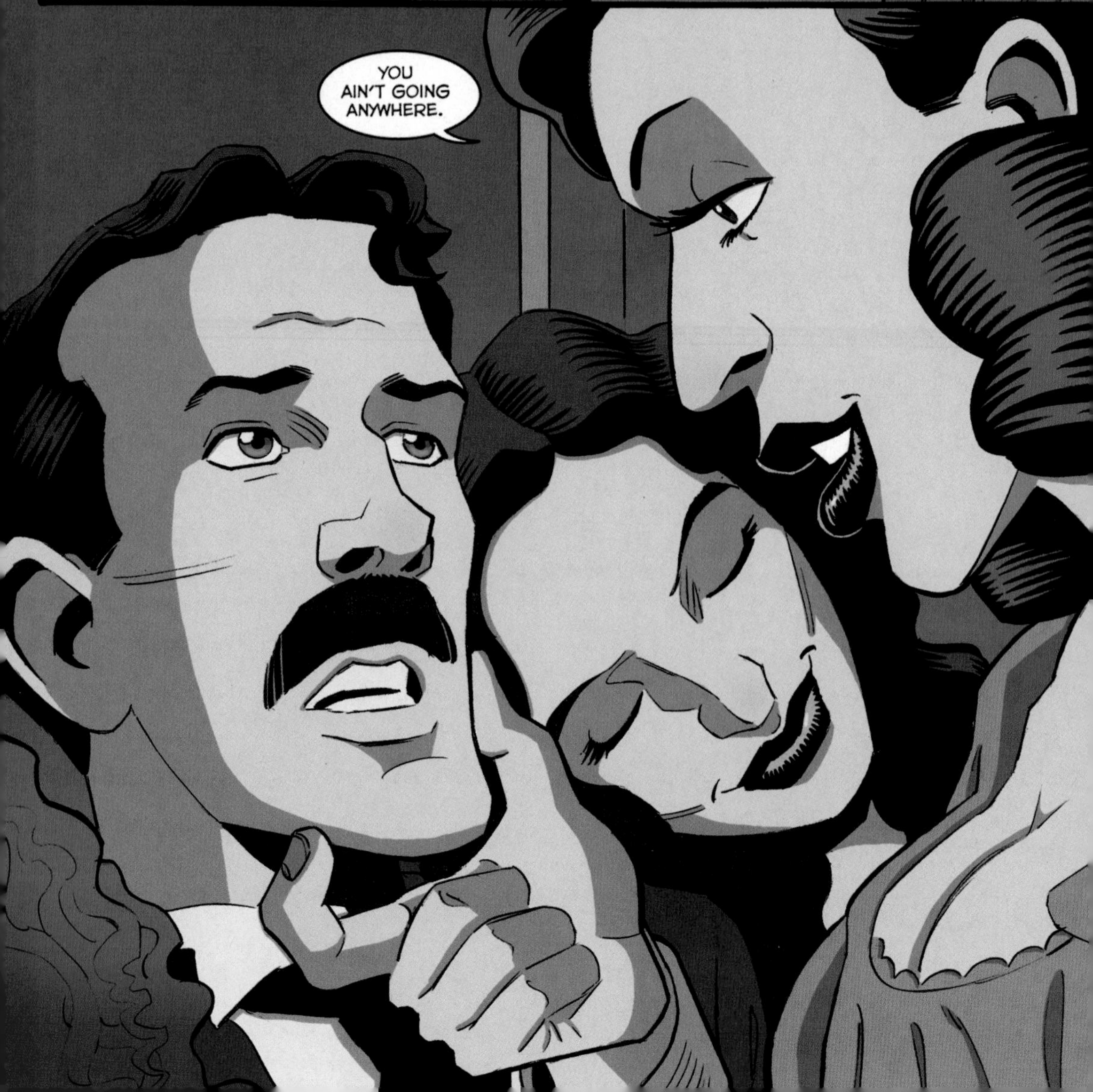
YOU AIN'T GOING ANYWHERE.

Email your letters and fan-art to
HeraldComic@gmail.com

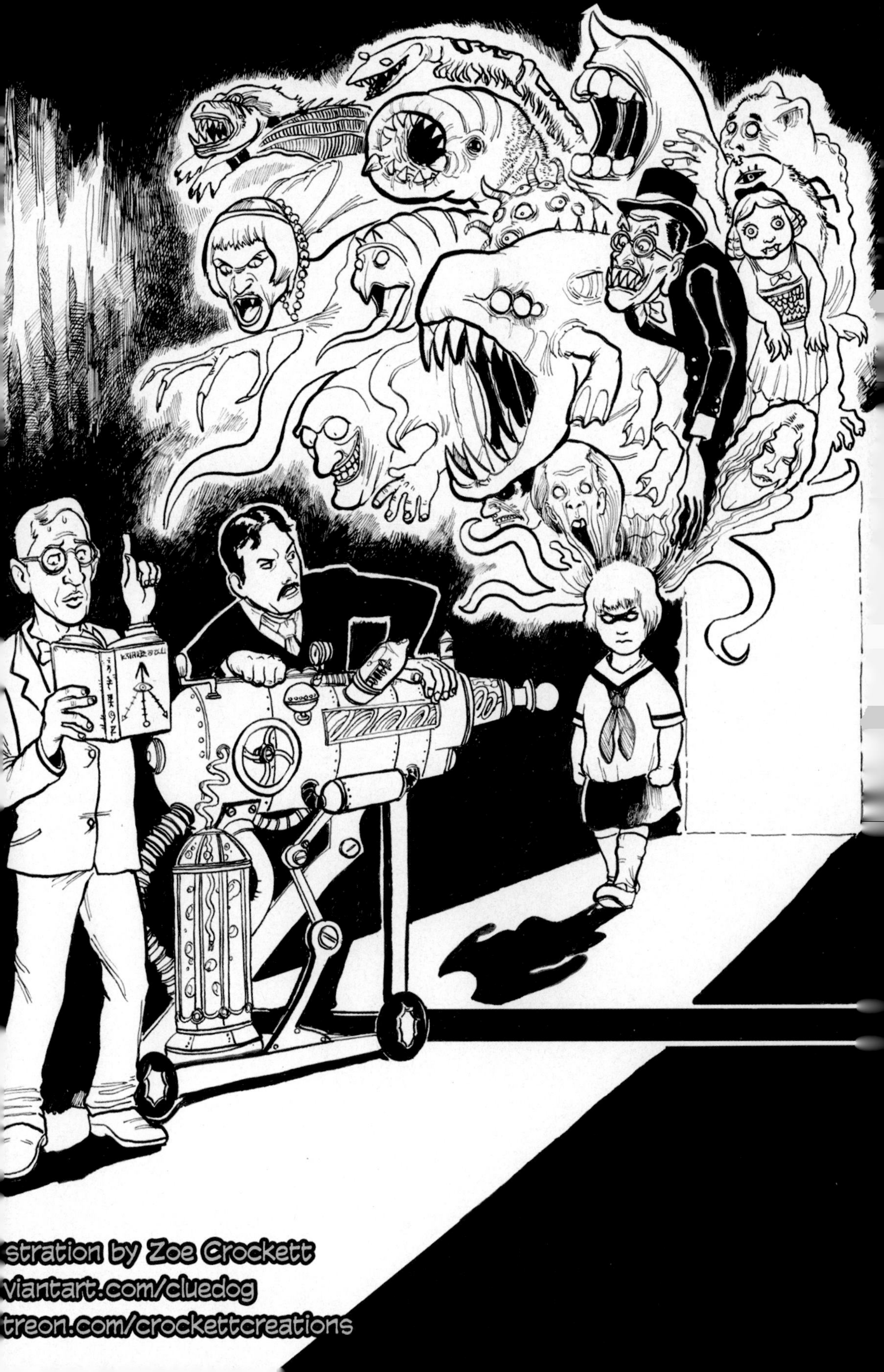
ᛕᛊᚺᚨᚱᛉ ᛟᛚᛚ

stration by Zoe Crockett
viantart.com/cluedog
treon.com/crockettcreations

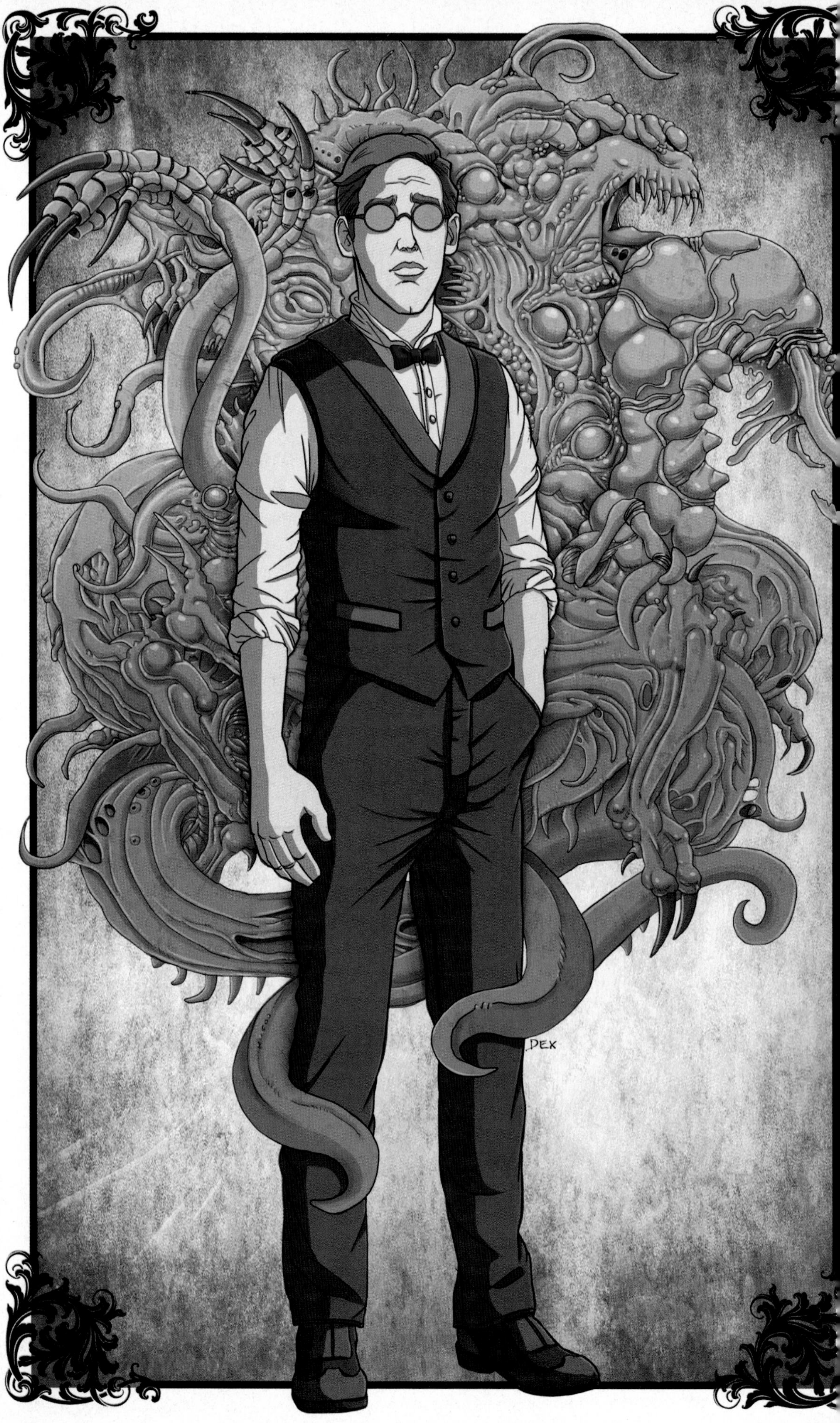
DEX

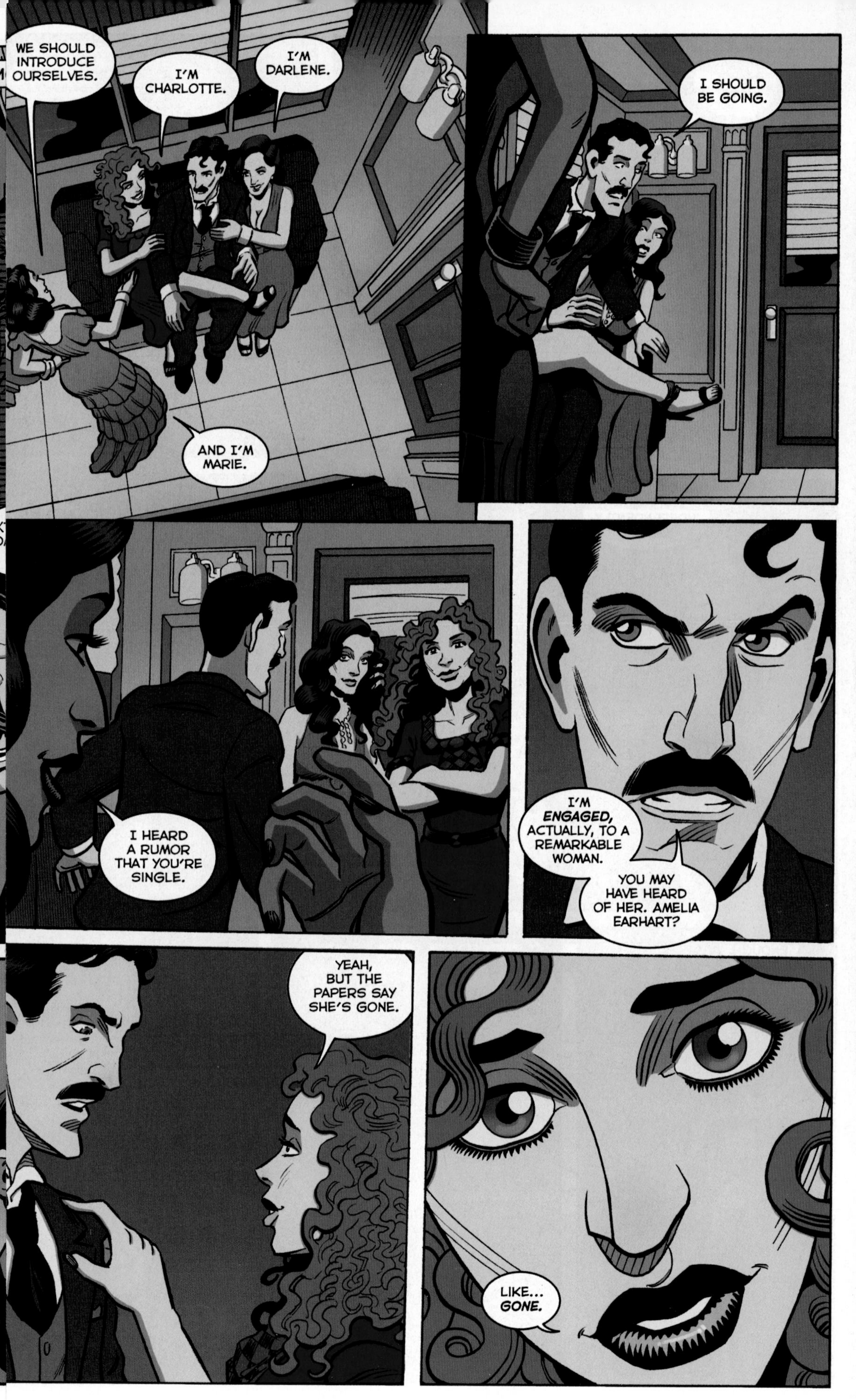

WE SHOULD INTRODUCE OURSELVES.
I'M CHARLOTTE.
I'M DARLENE.
AND I'M MARIE.
I SHOULD BE GOING.
I HEARD A RUMOR THAT YOU'RE SINGLE.
I'M *ENGAGED,* ACTUALLY, TO A REMARKABLE WOMAN.
YOU MAY HAVE HEARD OF HER. AMELIA EARHART?
YEAH, BUT THE PAPERS SAY SHE'S GONE.
LIKE... *GONE.*

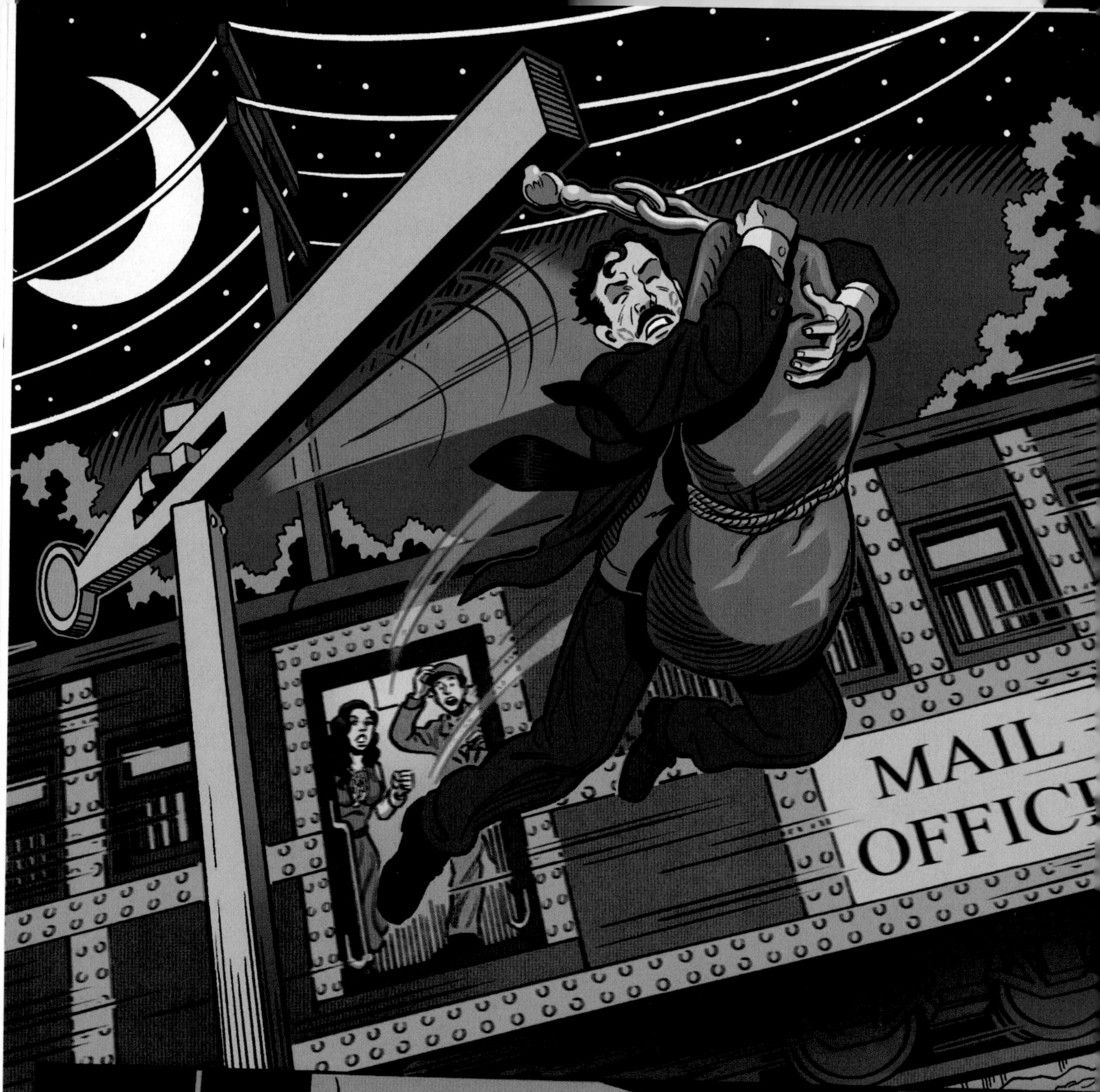
MAIL
OFFIC

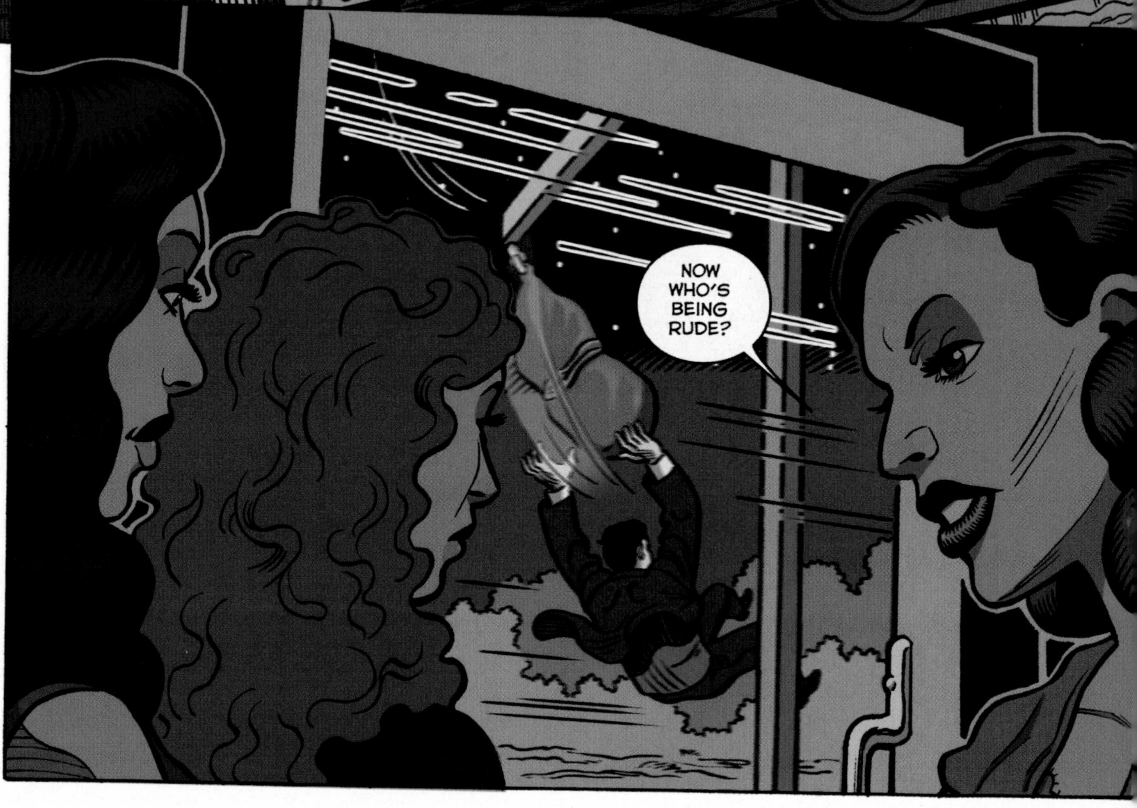
NOW WHO'S BEING RUDE?

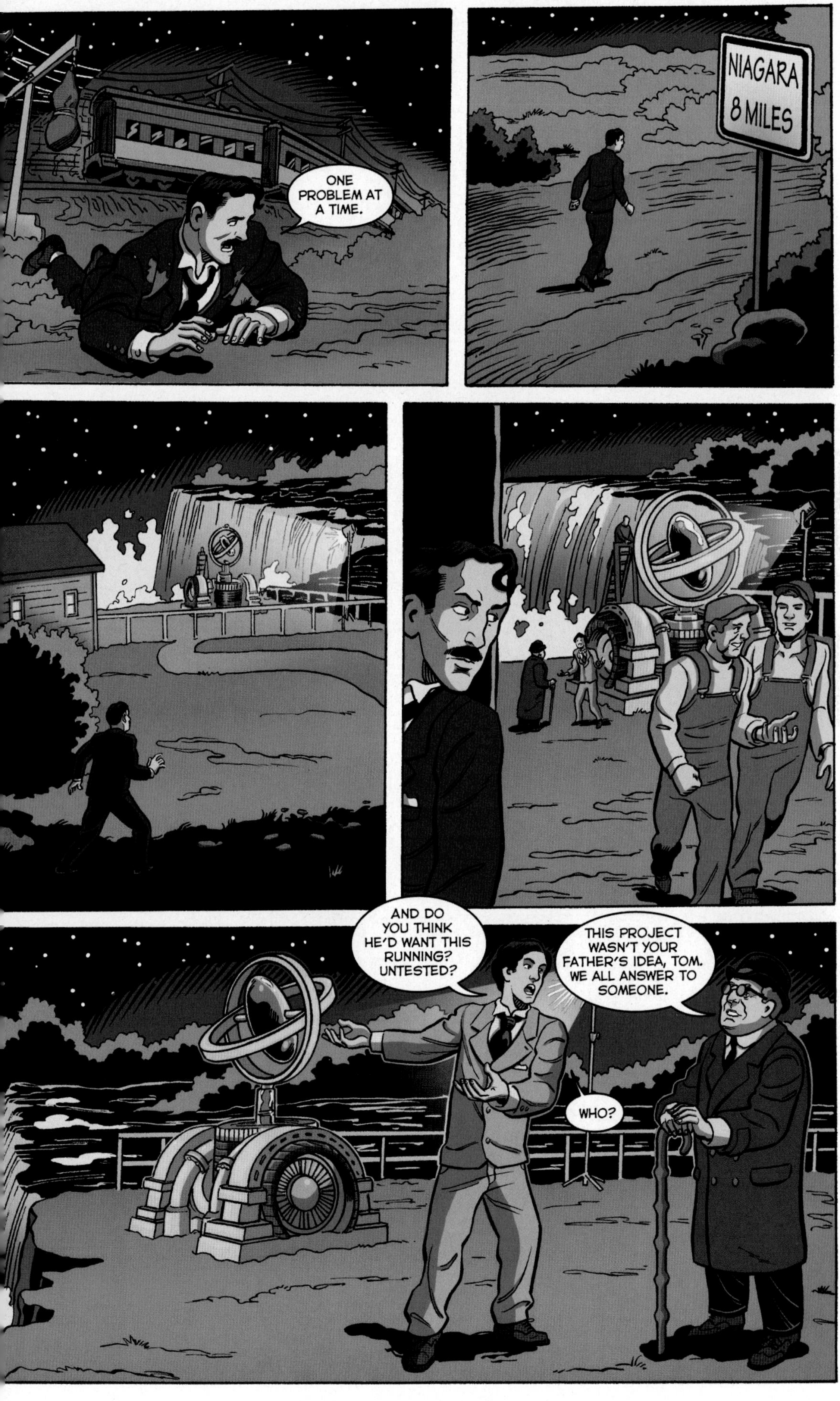
ONE PROBLEM AT A TIME.
NIAGARA 8 MILES
AND DO YOU THINK HE'D WANT THIS RUNNING? UNTESTED?
THIS PROJECT WASN'T YOUR FATHER'S IDEA, TOM. WE ALL ANSWER TO SOMEONE.
WHO?

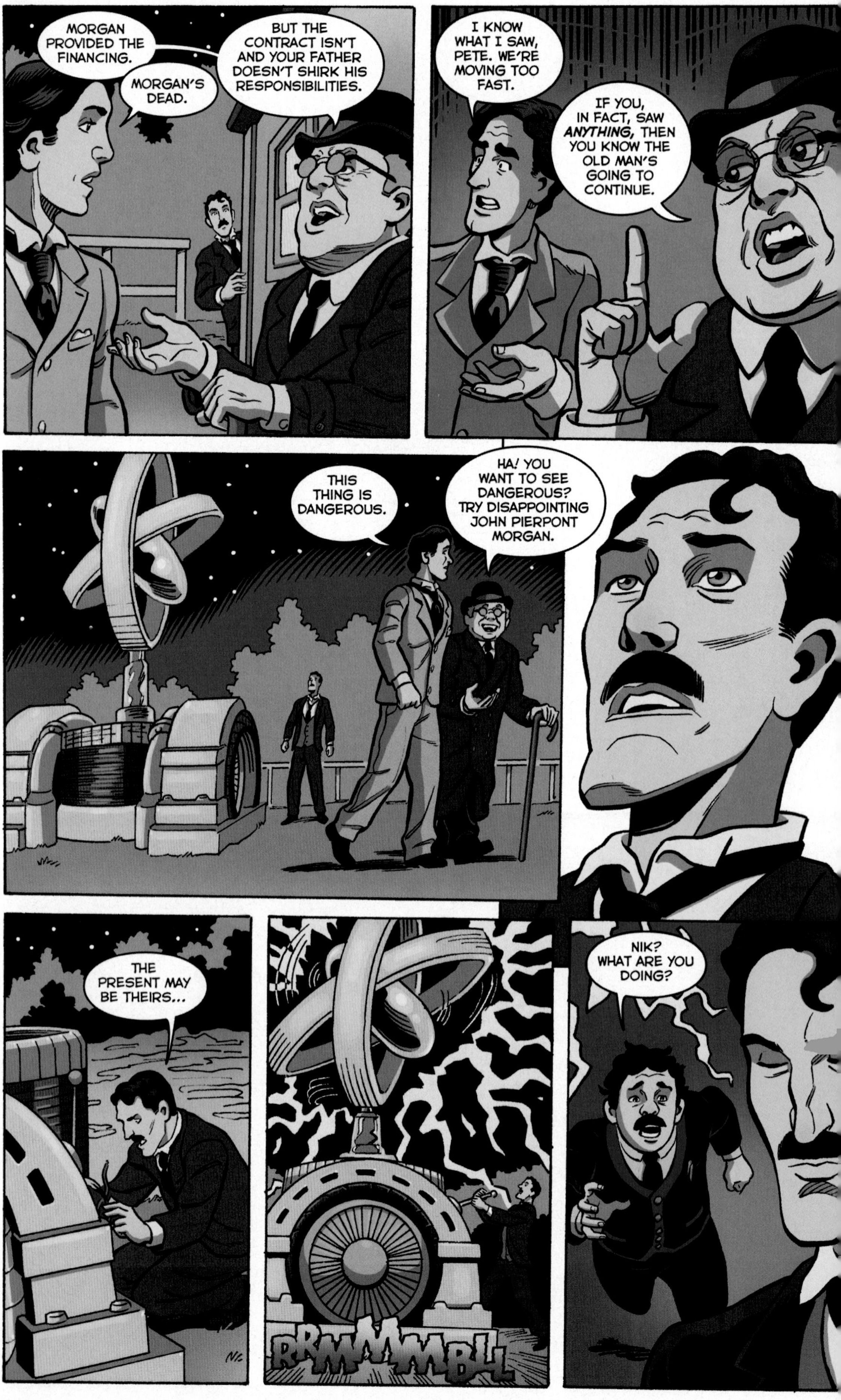
MORGAN PROVIDED THE FINANCING.
MORGAN'S DEAD.
BUT THE CONTRACT ISN'T AND YOUR FATHER DOESN'T SHIRK HIS RESPONSIBILITIES.
I KNOW WHAT I SAW, PETE. WE'RE MOVING TOO FAST.
IF YOU, IN FACT, SAW *ANYTHING,* THEN YOU KNOW THE OLD MAN'S GOING TO CONTINUE.
THIS THING IS DANGEROUS.
HA! YOU WANT TO SEE DANGEROUS? TRY DISAPPOINTING JOHN PIERPONT MORGAN.
THE PRESENT MAY BE THEIRS...
RRMMMMBLL
NIK? WHAT ARE YOU DOING?

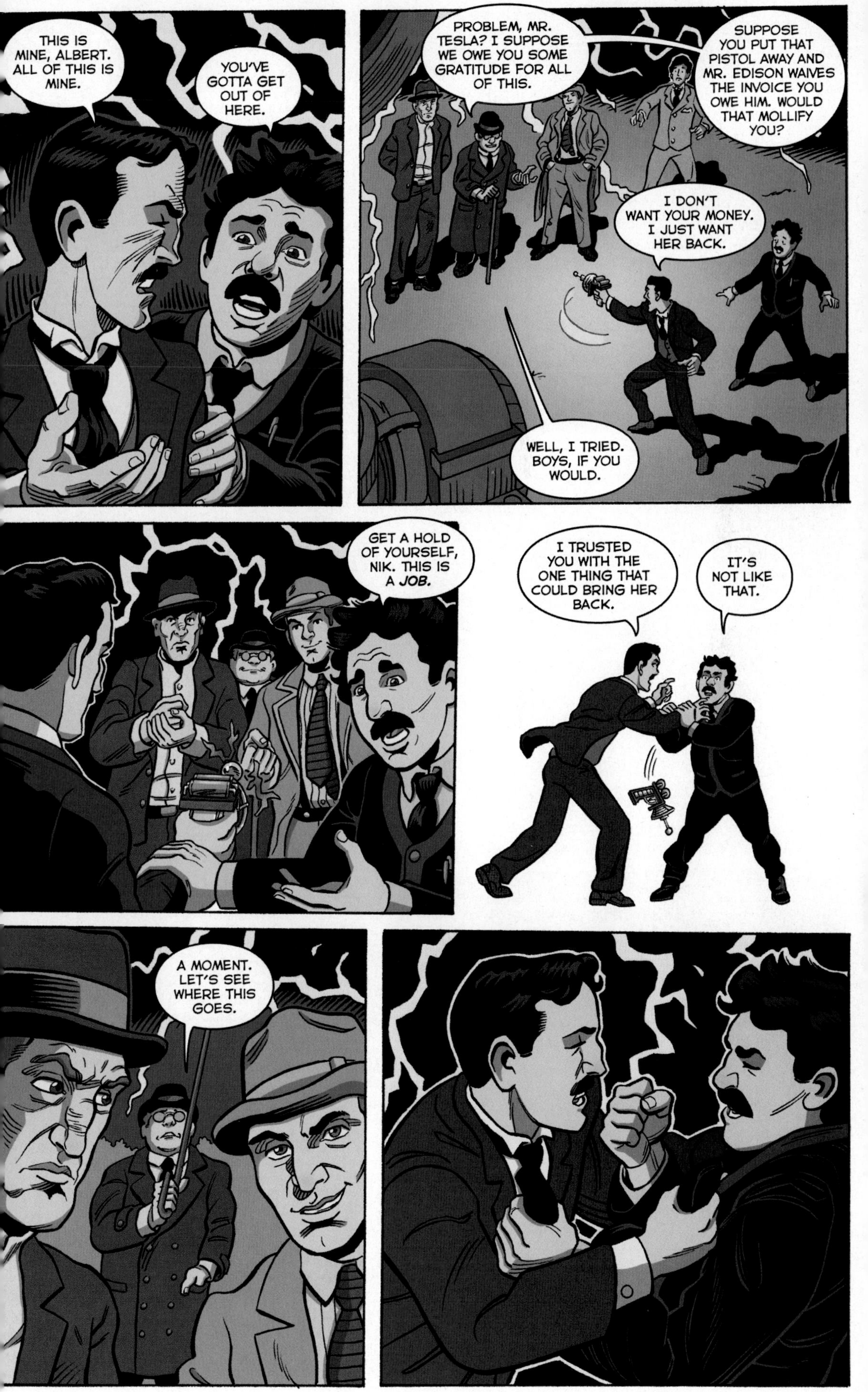
THIS IS MINE, ALBERT. ALL OF THIS IS MINE.
YOU'VE GOTTA GET OUT OF HERE.
PROBLEM, MR. TESLA? I SUPPOSE WE OWE YOU SOME GRATITUDE FOR ALL OF THIS.
SUPPOSE YOU PUT THAT PISTOL AWAY AND MR. EDISON WAIVES THE INVOICE YOU OWE HIM. WOULD THAT MOLLIFY YOU?
I DON'T WANT YOUR MONEY. I JUST WANT HER BACK.
WELL, I TRIED. BOYS, IF YOU WOULD.
GET A HOLD OF YOURSELF, NIK. THIS IS A *JOB.*
I TRUSTED YOU WITH THE ONE THING THAT COULD BRING HER BACK.
IT'S NOT LIKE THAT.
A MOMENT. LET'S SEE WHERE THIS GOES.

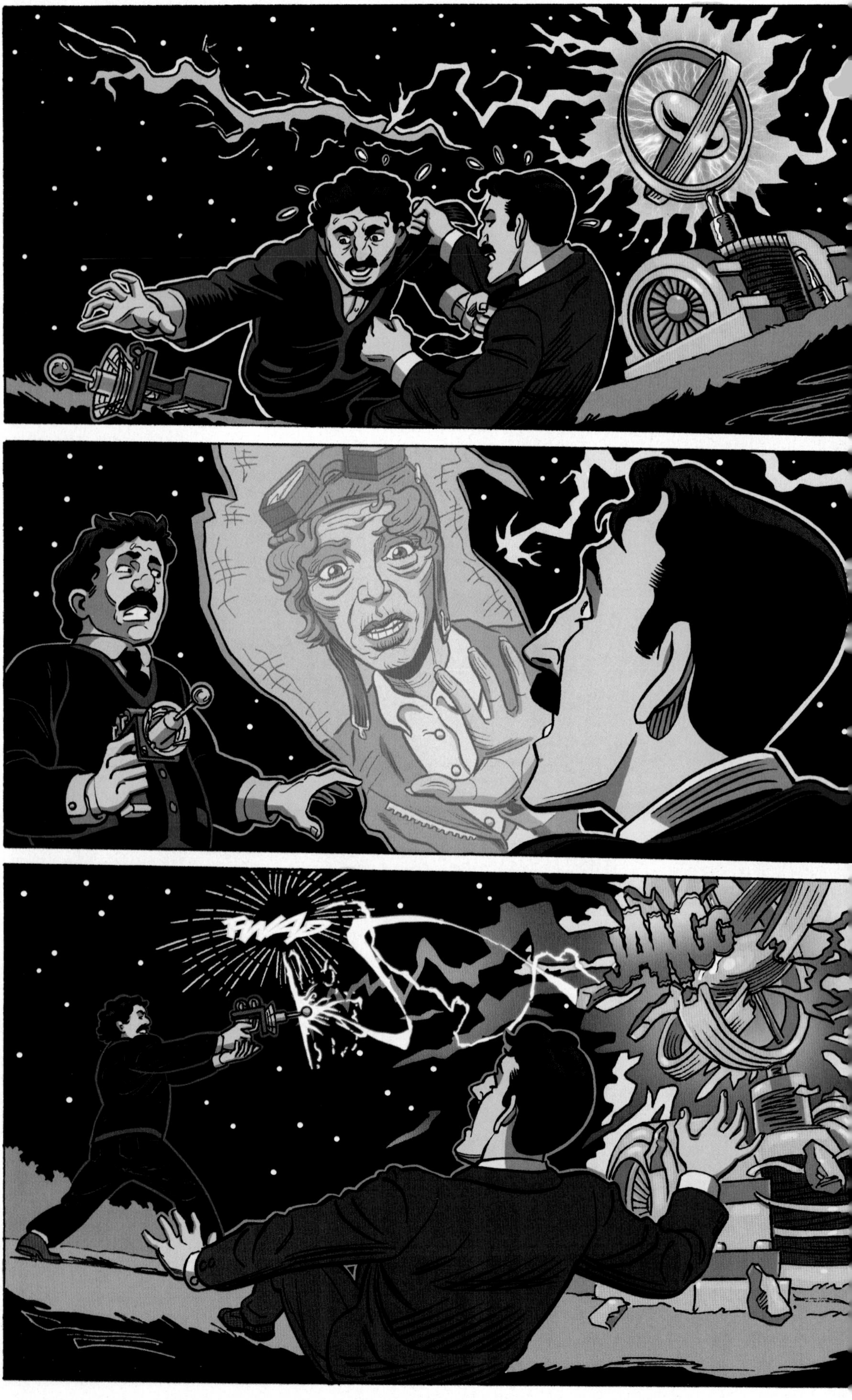

FWAP
JANGG

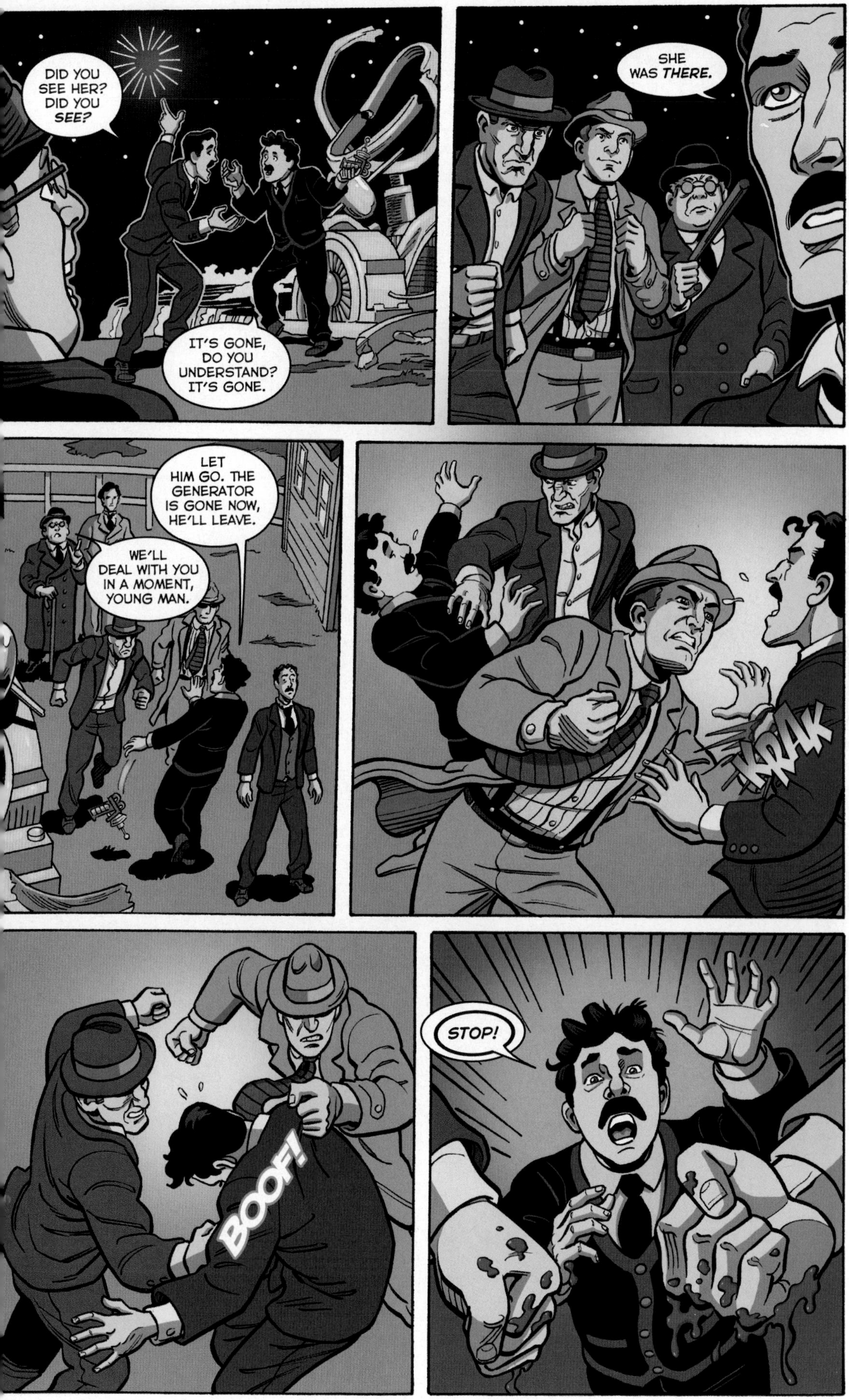
DID YOU SEE HER? DID YOU *SEE?*
IT'S GONE, DO YOU UNDERSTAND? IT'S GONE.
SHE WAS *THERE.*
LET HIM GO. THE GENERATOR IS GONE NOW, HE'LL LEAVE.
WE'LL DEAL WITH YOU IN A MOMENT, YOUNG MAN.
KRAK
BOOF!
STOP!

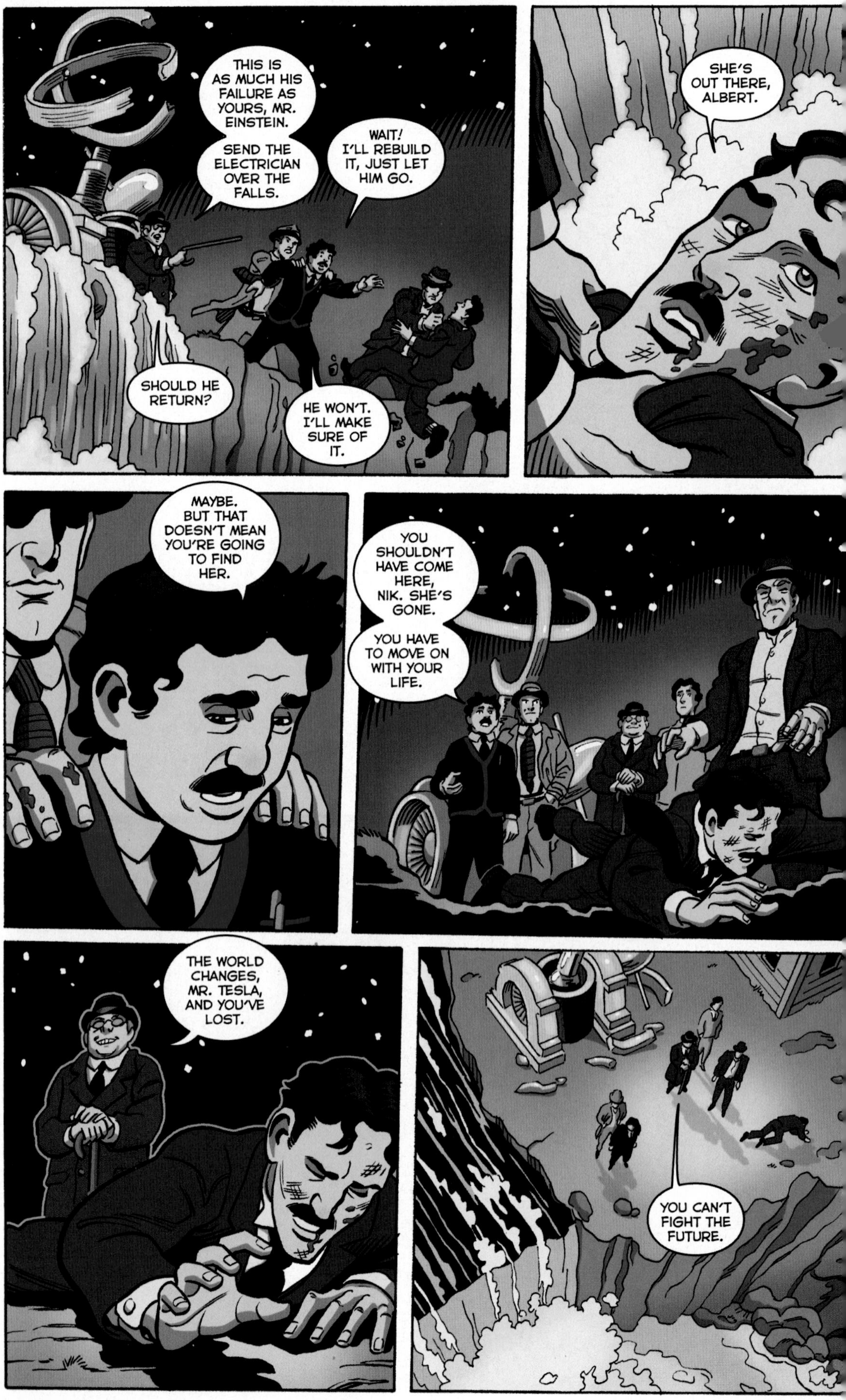
THIS IS AS MUCH HIS FAILURE AS YOURS, MR. EINSTEIN.
SEND THE ELECTRICIAN OVER THE FALLS.
WAIT! I'LL REBUILD IT, JUST LET HIM GO.
SHOULD HE RETURN?
HE WON'T. I'LL MAKE SURE OF IT.
SHE'S OUT THERE, ALBERT.
MAYBE. BUT THAT DOESN'T MEAN YOU'RE GOING TO FIND HER.
YOU SHOULDN'T HAVE COME HERE, NIK. SHE'S GONE.
YOU HAVE TO MOVE ON WITH YOUR LIFE.
THE WORLD CHANGES, MR. TESLA, AND YOU'VE LOST.
YOU CAN'T FIGHT THE FUTURE.

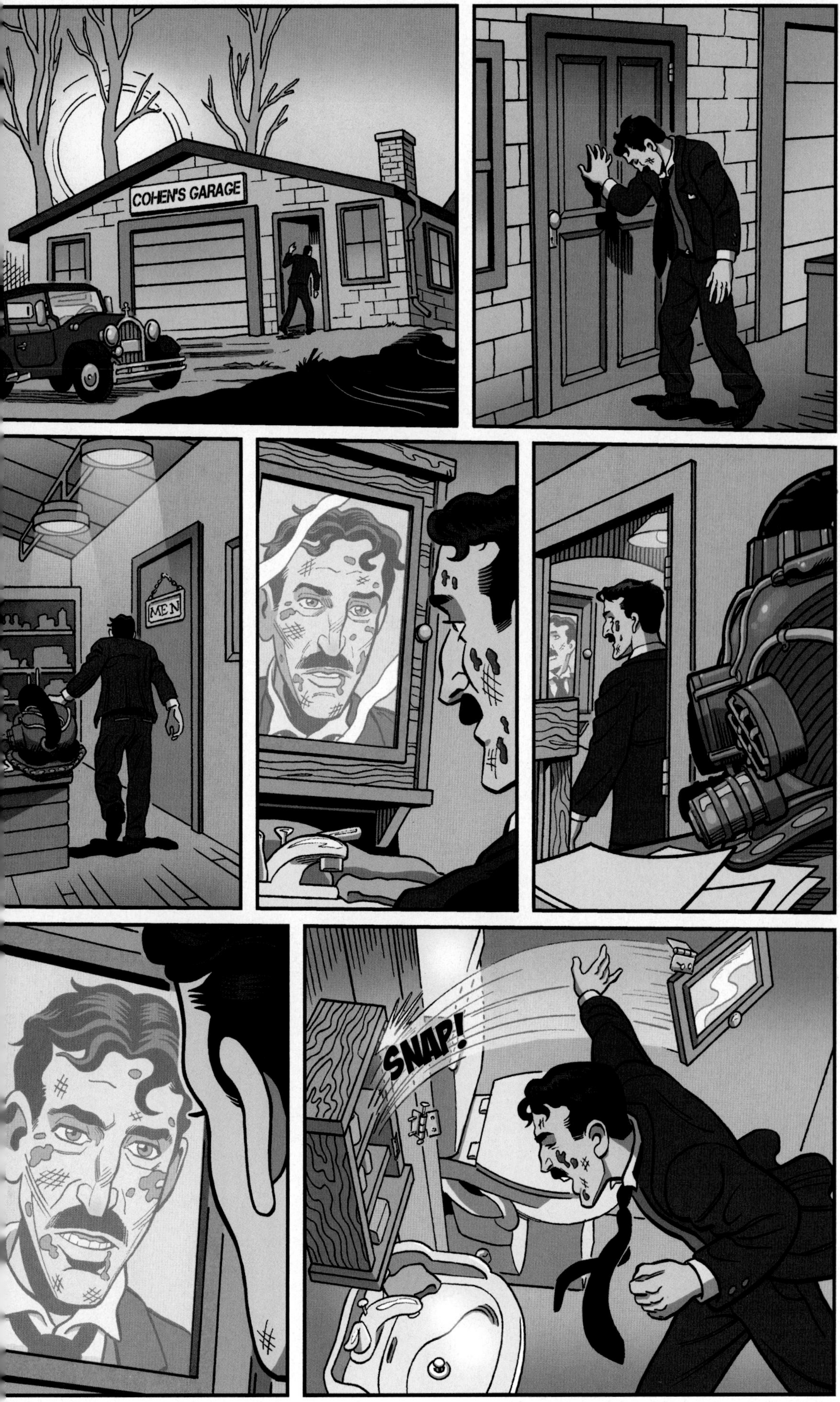
COHEN'S GARAGE
MEN
SNAP!

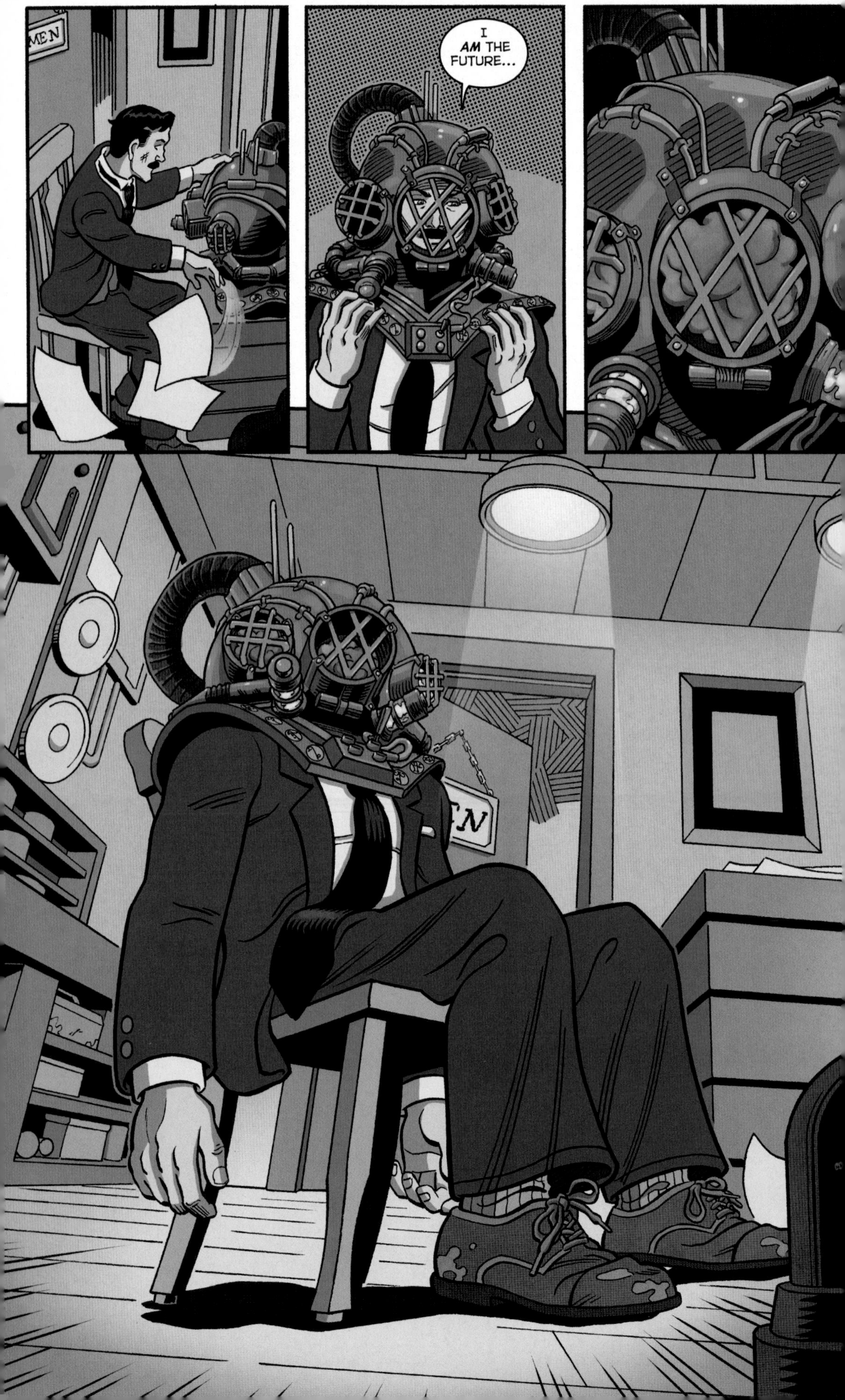
I AM THE FUTURE...
MEN
EN

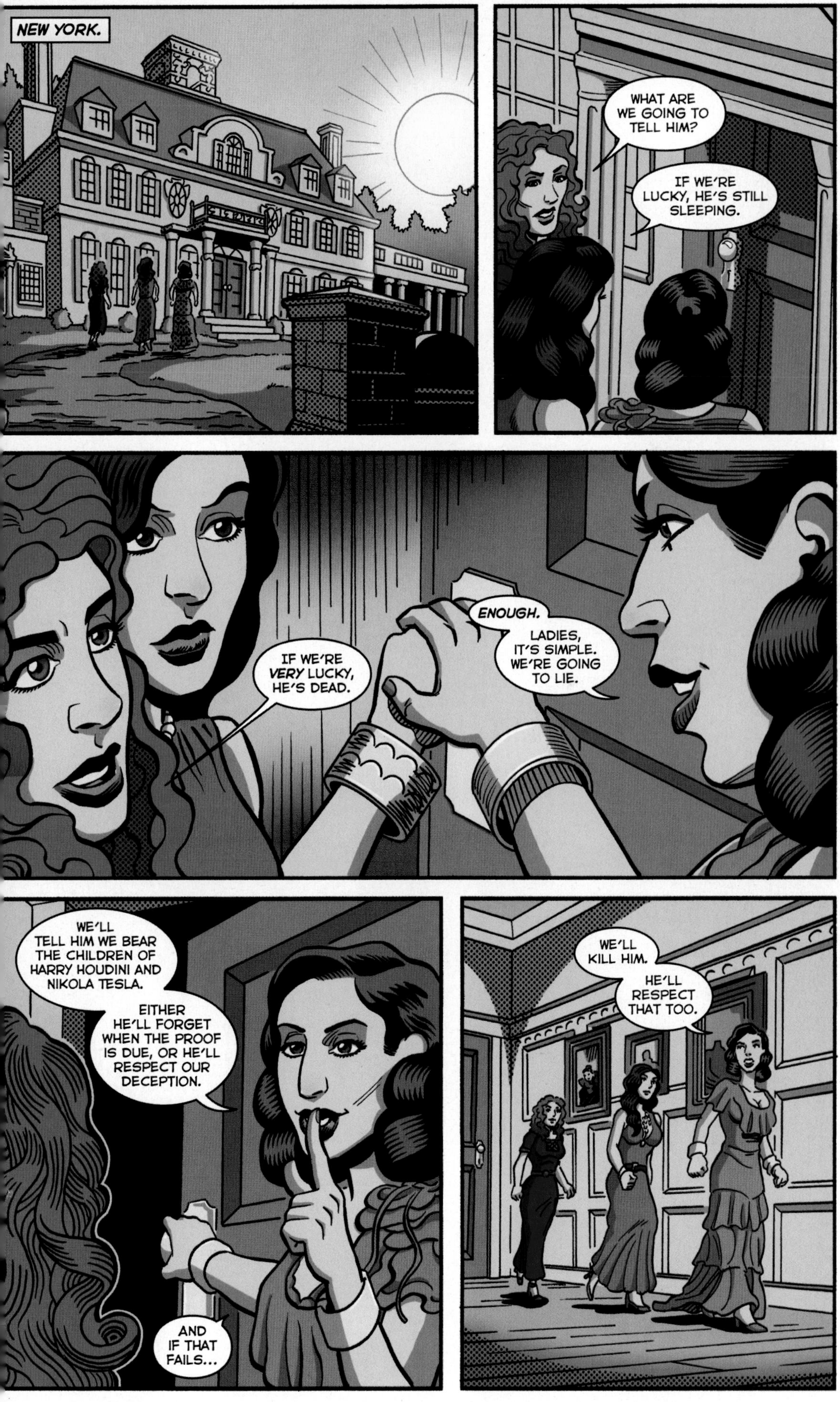
NEW YORK.
WHAT ARE WE GOING TO TELL HIM?
IF WE'RE LUCKY, HE'S STILL SLEEPING.
IF WE'RE VERY LUCKY, HE'S DEAD.
ENOUGH.
LADIES, IT'S SIMPLE. WE'RE GOING TO LIE.
WE'LL TELL HIM WE BEAR THE CHILDREN OF HARRY HOUDINI AND NIKOLA TESLA.
EITHER HE'LL FORGET WHEN THE PROOF IS DUE, OR HE'LL RESPECT OUR DECEPTION.
AND IF THAT FAILS...
WE'LL KILL HIM.
HE'LL RESPECT THAT TOO.

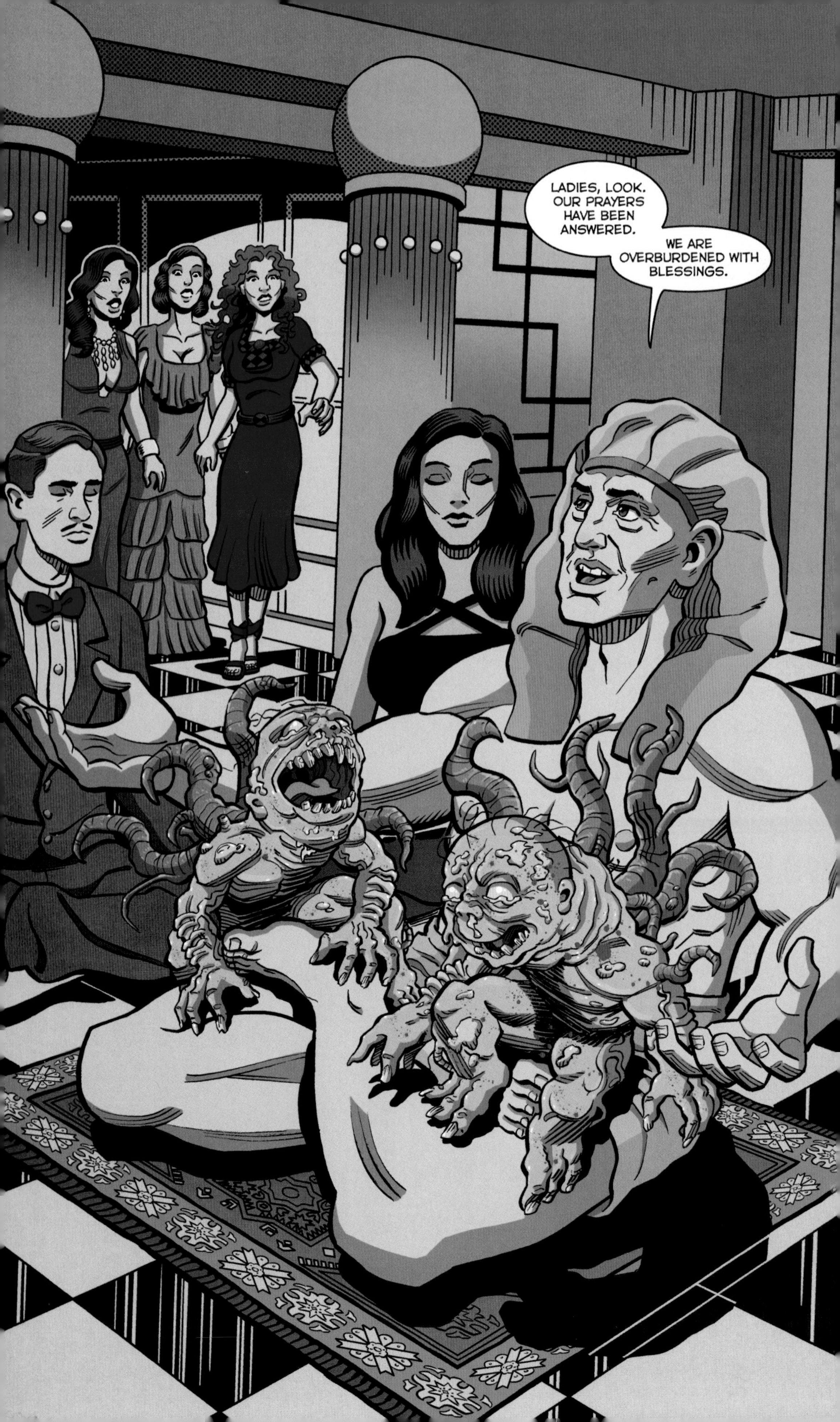
LADIES, LOOK. OUR PRAYERS HAVE BEEN ANSWERED.
WE ARE OVERBURDENED WITH BLESSINGS.

mail your letters and fan-art to
leraldComic@gmail.com

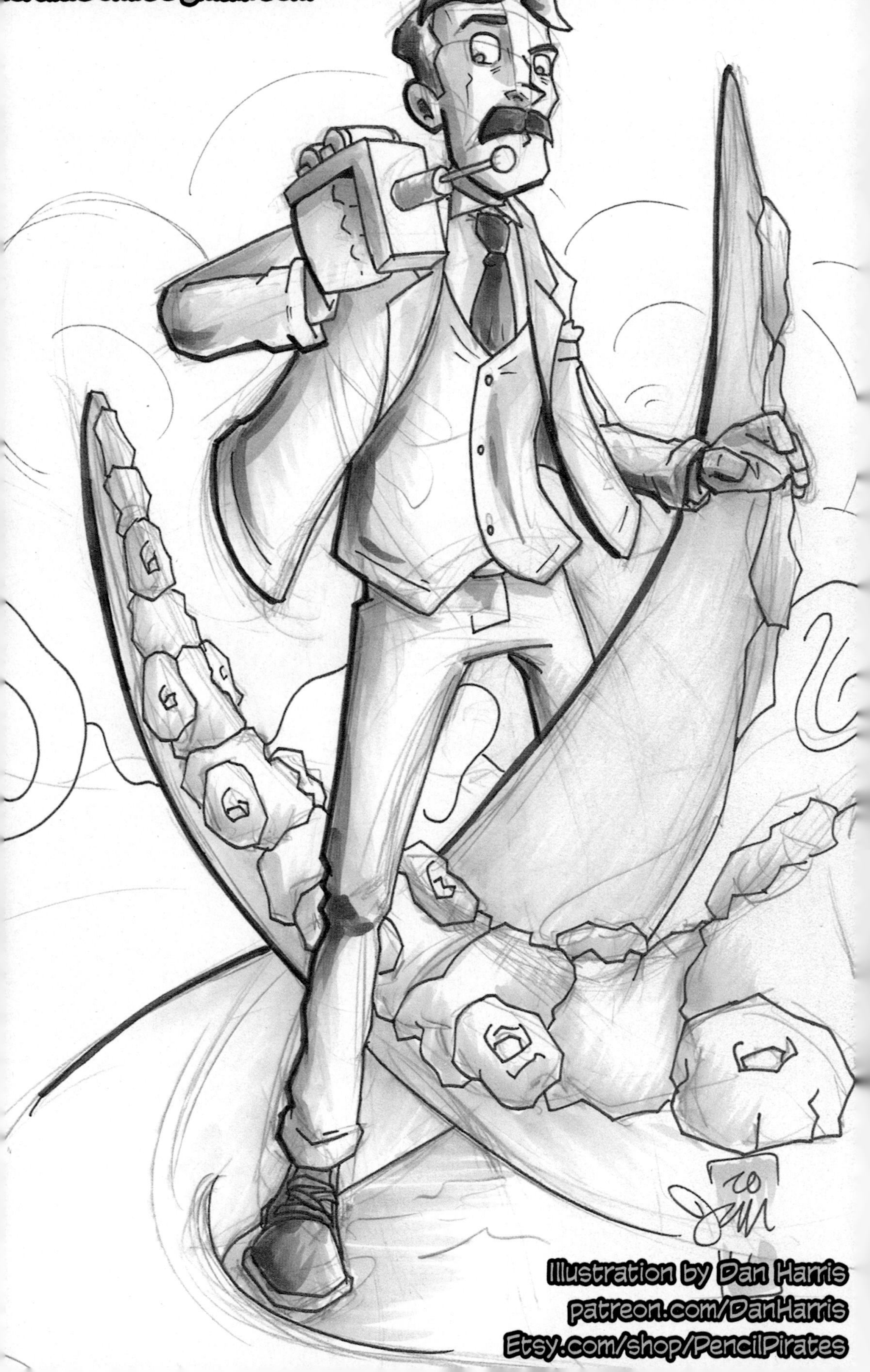

Illustration by Dan Harris
patreon.com/DanHarris
Etsy.com/shop/PencilPirates

PROCESS WORK

- Tom Rogers

CHECK OUT MORE
BEHIND-THE-SCENES ART AT
PATREON.COM/TOMROGERSCOMICS

HERE'S A QUICK PEEK AT THE MAKING OF PAGE 12. IN THIS PAGE, TESLA ESCAPES THE SCARLET SIRENS BY LEAPING OUT OF THE TRAIN AND SWINGING AROUND A MAIL DELIVERY POST.

JOHN SENT ME SOME PHOTO (AND VIDEO) REFERENCE OF THE MAIL CATCHER THING WHICH IS ALWAYS EXTREMELY APPRECIATED!

ANYWAYS, MY GOAL WITH THIS PAGE WAS TO MAKE THE TOP PANEL AS DYNAMIC AND CLEAR AS POSSIBLE WHILE KEEPING THE ACTION MOVING FROM LEFT TO RIGHT (FOLLOWING THE NATURAL COURSE OF THE READER'S EYE.)

THE MAIL DELIVERY POST WAS ESTABLISHED IN THE LAST PANEL OF THE PREVIOUS PAGE:

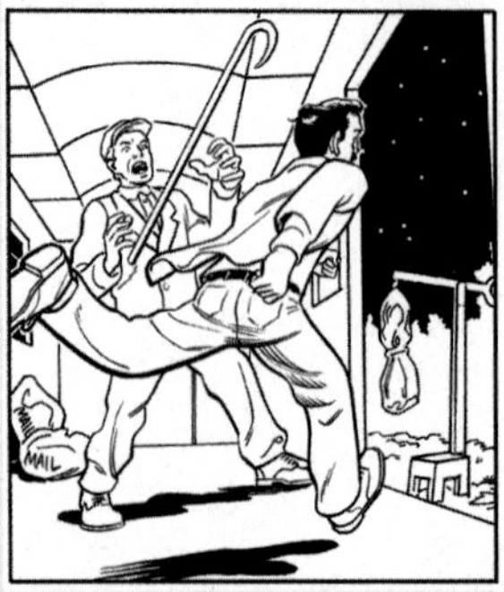
MAIL

STEP 1:
THUMBNAIL/LAYOUT

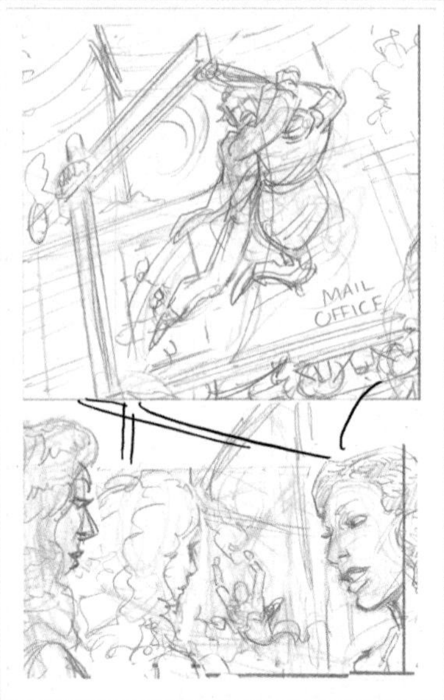
MAIL
OFFICE

STEP 2:
PENCILS

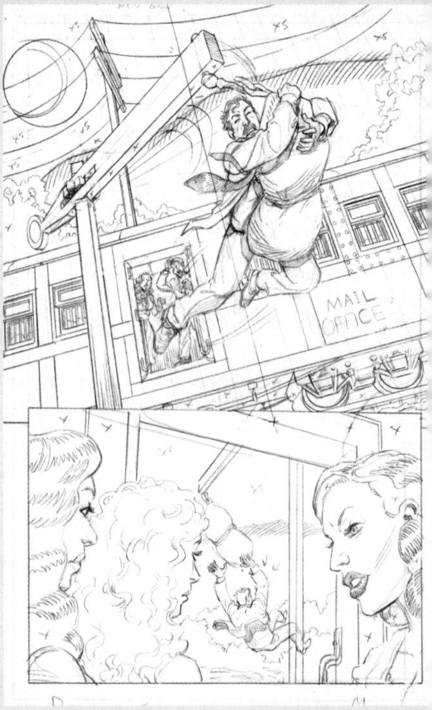
MAIL
OFFICE

BY THE WAY, THE GUY WORKING IN THE MAIL CAR HAS THAT LONG HOOK TO SNAG THE BAG OF MAIL AS THE TRAIN PASSES. (DID YOU KNOW THAT? I SURE DIDN'T! WORKING ON HERALD IS A VERY EDUCATIONAL EXPERIENCE!) ANYWAYS, I'M GETTING DE-RAILED HERE (TRAIN PUNS)!

AFTER FINISHING THE PENCILS (WHICH I CAN KEEP LOOSER WHEN INKING MY OWN WORK), I CONTINUED ON TO THE INKS! USUALLY, DEX COLORS RIGHT OVER MY PENCILS, BUT I HAD A HANKERING TO INK THIS ISSUE AFTER DISCOVERING ZEBRA BRUSH PENS (I HIGHLY RECOMMEND!) WHICH I USED TO INK THE CHARACTERS. THE RULED LINES AND BACKGROUND WERE INKED WITH FABER CASTELL ("F" AND "M" SIZE) PITT ARTIST PENS.

WHILE THIS WAS CERTAINLY A FUN EXPERIMENT, I'LL PROBABLY BE GOING BACK TO TIGHT PENCILS (RATHER THAN INKS) FOR THE NEXT ISSUE SINCE THIS ONE DEFINITELY TOOK LONGER TO COMPLETE THAN USUAL.

ANYWAYS, I HOPE YOU GOT A KICK OUT OF THIS LATEST INSTALLMENT IN TOM'S COMICS CORNER!

KEEP ON TRUCKIN'!

-TOM

STEP 3:
INKS

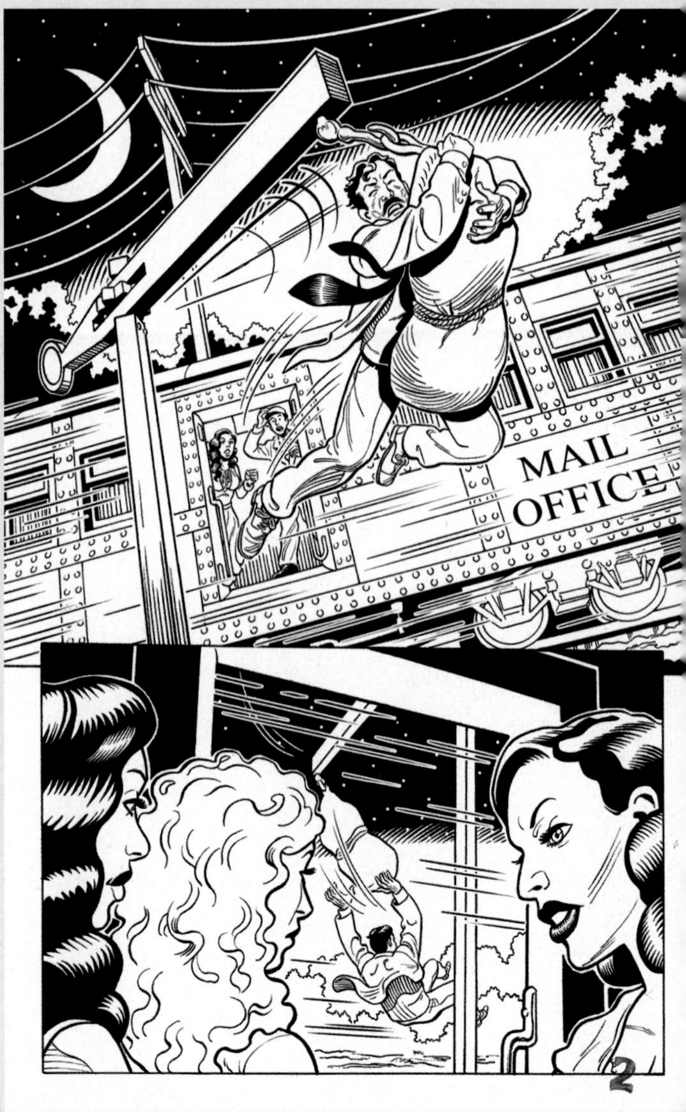
MAIL
OFFICE

STEP 4: ***COLORS BY DEXTER WEEKS***

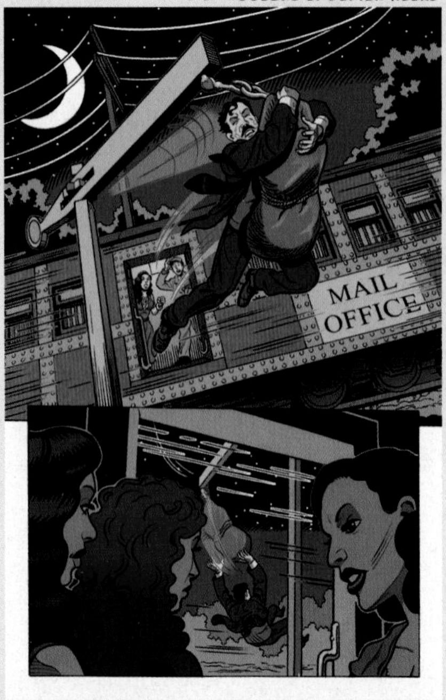
MAIL
OFFICE